SNOW, SLEDS
& SILENCE

SNOW, SLEDS & SILENCE

The Story of the Nordkapp Expedition

RONA CANT

First published in 2011 by Libri Publishing

Copyright © Rona Cant

ISBN 978 1 907471 19 3

A CIP catalogue record for this book is available from The British Library

All photographs by Rona Cant unless otherwise acknowledged

Front cover design by Helen Taylor

Page design by Carnegie Publishing

Front cover photo by C. O'Dowd

Printed in the UK by Ashford Colour Press

Libri Publishing
Brunel House
Volunteer Way
Faringdon
Oxfordshire
SN7 7YR

Tel: +44 (0)845 873 3837

www.libripublishing.co.uk

Acknowledgements

Serendipity happens to all of us at some time in our lives. For some it makes no difference; for others, life is changed forever. Why is that? Often it is because it comes at the right time in someone's life, when they're prepared to take a chance. I have had several serendipitous moments in my life and this expedition was the result of one of them.

In 2000–1, I took part in the BT Global Challenge Round the World Yacht Race. On my return, I went back to Southampton to work on the yachts for the summer – I knew that I could not just walk away. At the end of September, I returned home and wrote my first book, *A Challenge Too Far?*, about my experience of the yacht race. However, I had only planned to do the race and then write the book; I had nothing planned for what would happen when I finished the book. Then I bumped into a friend of mine, Heidi Kurtz, in Oxford, who told me she was to take part in a Charity Challenge where, if she raised enough money, she would get to sled in Lapland. The rest, as they say, is history. My sincere thanks must go to Heidi, who not only gave me a plan and a project but opened up a whole new world of interest for me which continues to this day.

My first contact at Cancer Research UK was Claire Bewell, now Claire Kelley, who was a tower of strength when it came to keeping me on track to raise the necessary funds to accomplish my goal. My thanks must go to all those who contributed – you are a part of this book.

I must also mention National Grid: I was working as a temp for them at the time, putting in long hours – by mutual consent as they needed the work completed and I needed the money! They matched the amount I'd raised for the event, without which I would not have made it to the start line.

You will see when you read the book that my children, Nicola and Simon (now grown up) are used to the life I now lead. They have always been a very strong support team for me, picking me up when I am down and putting me back into place when I have 'grown' too much! They are a continual source of delight for me and without them my world would be a much greyer place.

My fellow sledders on the Charity Challenge opened my eyes to a totally different world of win–win: I do hope you are all still having fun and raising lots of money for charity – I salute you. It was a joy to know you and sled with you. Paul, you were my knight in shining armour, coming to my rescue when my superman powers failed miserably.

Andru, I must give you a special thank you as you came up with the great title of *Snow, Sleds & Silence*. This just said it all to me, especially once I was on the Nordkapp Expedition and it turned out to be exactly that. Very many thanks – I think it is a great title.

On the last day of that challenge, if I had sat in a different seat on our final night's celebratory meal this book would not have been written because I would not have had that conversation with Per Thore and, who knows, the Nordkapp Expedition may not have taken place.

Per Thore has become a good friend and we have found a way to work together to help other people achieve their goals in the corporate world, and at a different level for those at University and at School (see Appendix 1) through the Arctic Leadership Challenges. He is a quiet but strong man and I feel totally safe when he is around. I am so pleased I met him. His wife, Hege, is phenomenal. She never seemed to stop working when we were preparing for the expedition and I know that she would dearly have loved to have been with us. Hege, now you can read what it was like! Their son little Jomar was not left out. He still had his run in the sled and would show us how he too could sled, even though he was only two and a half at the time. I hope he is not embarrassed by this.

A chance meeting also meant that a colleague of mine, Cathy, came along with us. She decided that she would like to film the expedition and, although I understand and know why, I have to say that I was not sorry when the Kautokeino river decided filming had to end. Luckily Ryno's filming at the start was back in the UK before the river made its decision. She was also keen to use a publicist and so Alex Foley and Anna Thomsen came on board to raise the media's awareness of us and what we were doing.

T4 Cameras Ltd came to our rescue before we left home for the Nordkapp Expedition by having enough of the right sort of batteries to charge the technical equipment so that Cathy could update the website and we could make the PR calls when required. We are indebted to you.

I have to mention Ryno, Hege's cousin. He worked tirelessly for us and would dearly have loved to have come on the expedition; but he did the hard graft of helping us get underway, filming in difficult conditions, driving to the

Nordkapp on his own and then driving all the way home with the rest of our team – a lot of work. Without him, we might still be out there. Thank you so much Ryno.

It was serendipity again when I decided that I should go to the Oxford Literary Festival as I had an idea for a novel and wanted to get some insights into how to go about it. There I met Clive Bloom, a literary agent, who has made the publication of this book possible by putting me in touch with Libri. Thank you – I believe chance meetings are invaluable. Another thank you must go to Celia, my publisher, whom I met over lunch as we discussed the contract and how to work together. Thank you for having faith in this book and I look forward to working with you to make it a success for both of us.

Big thanks have to go to my friends, Clare McKinley and Pete Lawrence, who took on the gargantuan task of reading the original manuscript and providing me with their opinion. I knew that they would both tell me what they thought with no holds barred, which is invaluable – so thank you to you both.

I had to get permission from my fellow sledders on the Charity Challenge to use the photos and talk about what happened along the way. Strangely, people seem to move house and change email addresses and it has been a challenge to contact them all. Across the Divide, who organised the trail for Cancer Research UK, have been extremely helpful and I know that Claire Langford has been searching in attics and through databases to try to find the four errant sledders who seem to have disappeared into the abyss. Claire, you deserve a medal for the effort you have made.

Last and certainly not least, to you the reader, thank you for picking up this book. I hope that you get a greater insight into what expeditions are really like – the highs, the lows and the 'I wish I wasn't here!' parts, as well as the 'WOW – that was such fun'. I hope you enjoy reading about the amazing Arctic Circle and life in a different culture. Being there and getting to understand the place, the different way of living and how the Sámi live at one with the environment was incredibly valuable.

Most of all I hope you enjoy reading about our expedition. Thank you for buying the book.

Rona

Contents

Foreword

The experienced mushers of Norway thought it was not possible to do this dog-sled trail. I kept hearing this so I looked at the map and I thought it's no problem. There were some difficult places and the mountains would be difficult but I felt it could be done.

I contacted Rona, who I met when she was on a Charity Challenge for Cancer Research UK that I guided and where we had been confronted with a number of challenges – including a whiteout – which she was able to overcome. However, I knew that she was prepared to go the extra mile when I found her feeding 70 dogs on her own, so I felt she would be able to cope with this Expedition. But this one would be much harder and would require a lot more grit and determination than the Charity Challenge.

Rona and Cathy arrived only a few days before we were about to set off so they were able to help with all the last-minute preparations. I had not met Cathy before but relied on Rona's judgement in inviting her along. There was a lot of work to do. As there were only three of us on this Expedition we would be working with sleds weighing 120 kilos each, not easy to pick up when they went over. However, the girls managed to deal with this challenge and others very well, except on the odd occasion when I had to help out.

This Expedition would be a race against time. We had to have a late start because we needed the road to Nordkapp to be open so that the dogs and sleds could be collected and taken home. If the road was not open we would have to turn round and sled back again. The road opened the day we arrived! The last couple of days before the last camp were very difficult as we had no snow. We were getting nearer to the sea. This added to the difficulty of the trail as we were near the Gulf Stream.

The trail was a challenge for the dogs, it was really tough for them. It was the end of a busy season and although they were trained they still had their winter fur so they were too hot, making it even more difficult with the fluctuating temperatures. The trail was tough for all of us. There was a lot of work to do. On the trail you have to focus on the things you need to do. There is no time to talk about how you feel. You have to concentrate on navigating the route through unknown terrain over ice, snow and rocks in very difficult conditions.

On top of that you have to find a suitable campsite (hopefully with access to water), then everyone has to help prepare the dogs' food, feed them, set up camp and cook the food for the humans. In the morning you have to load the sled and clear the campsite (including the dogs' faeces); by the time you have done this every day you are tired and go to bed so that you are ready to do it all over again the next day.

When we arrived at Nordkapp it made me very happy and I was proud of what the dogs had done and of what we had done – we did a fantastic job in ten days.   It's when you get home that you think about the terrain and the mountains and you get the true feeling of what you have done. They said it couldn't be done – but we did it.

Per Thore Hansen
Arctic Expedition Leader
Norway, 2011

Photo: C. O'Dowd

MAP OF THE ROUTE

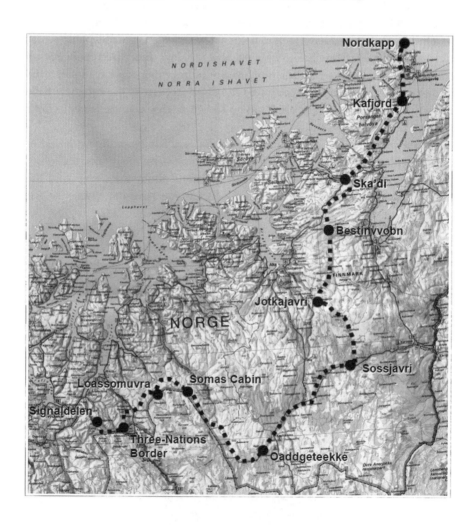

The experienced mushers of Norway said it was impossible: they said that the sleds were too heavy; they said we couldn't start from Signaldalen as the sleds would not be able to withstand the trail through the forest and would be broken within two days; they said that Cathy and I were too inexperienced to do the trail, as Per Thore wanted to take us over the Haalti Mountains. They thought he was crazy to try.

But Per Thore believed it could be done. He believed the sleds would withstand the punishment they would take and he believed that Cathy and I could do it. So, on 10 April 2004, the three of us set off to dog-sled over 500 kilometres to Nordkapp, the northernmost tip of Norway, to do a trail that had never been done before.

This is the story of how the Nordkapp Expedition turned from a dream into reality; and how a Norwegian dog-sled racer, a British round-the-world yachtswoman and a South African mountaineer, took up the challenge to prove 'them' wrong.

Rona

CHAPTER 1

How It All Began

So let me start at the beginning. It was a lovely spring day in March 2002 when I bumped into Heidi Kurtz. She was a graduate at St Peter's College, Oxford, where I had worked before giving up a nine-to-five job for a life of uncertainty, travel and some danger. At that particular moment I had no plans for what I should do, I was in limbo. Heidi, in contrast, was very excited as she had just signed up to take part in a Charity Challenge for Cancer Research UK. If she raised enough money she would go dog-sledding in Lapland! Too late, a fizz of electricity had zapped through my skull and I wanted to know more. Heidi, her face and voice full of excitement at the anticipated adventure, explained what the challenge was. 'Wow, that sounds romantic and exciting', I cried. 'I'd love to do that.' A flicker of a look dashed across her face, a look of regret that she had ever mentioned it, I thought. But I'm afraid I was oblivious, I could not wait to get home to sign up myself.

I managed to raise the money and, in March 2003, off I went into the Arctic Circle. Was it romantic? Exciting? Far from it. In fact, I got off the sled at the end of the trail saying 'Done that, been there – NEVER again', only to find myself 24-hours later at our farewell dinner sitting next to Per Thore, who had been our guide on that trail, saying to him 'What is it that you would really like to do?' He told me about a trail that his friend, Tom Frode Johanson, had tried to open but had only managed to do part of it. It was a trail to dog-sled from north of Tromsø to the northernmost tip of Norway, the Nordkapp. He told me that the experienced mushers of Norway thought it was impossible; but Per Thore believed it could be done. It would be a new route in Europe's last wilderness, a route that he could use to lead other adventurous people dog-sledding. It would bring a new dimension to his business.

Having done the BT Global Challenge in 2000, I felt that those who embarked on the original British Steel Global Challenge (the same race with a different title sponsor) in 1992 were the true pioneers. As Per Thore said 'the experienced mushers of Norway thought it was impossible' that fizz of electricity went through my head again – I wanted to be a part something that had not been done before. I wanted to experience that same pioneering spirit.

Now, some may say that it was the ten vodka cocktails I had drunk at the Ice Palace the night before; or alternatively, it may have been riding across the frozen lake on a snow-mobile and seeing a ten-dog sled skimming over the ice, actually being used as a vehicle and not just a tourist attraction or for a challenge. Whatever it was, something made me feel that I wanted to get back on a sled – but one that wasn't being held up by the sled in front – facing a real challenge, something with a far more difficult goal than that we had just accomplished.

What does a little time do to us? As the meal ended I heard myself saying to Per Thore 'Well if you decide to go ahead, let me know because I might very well be interested in coming along.' I couldn't believe I had said it, part of me was looking around for this 'other' person. It's strange what happens when you get outside your comfort zone and achieve your goal. Whatever happened to 'Done that, been there – NEVER again'?

The idea had definitely struck a chord with me. Was it the idea of the open wilderness, far more deserted than the countryside we had been through? Was it the thought of the almost total silence, with only the whoosh of the sleds as they were pulled across the snow and the pitter-patter of the dogs' paws running? Was it the challenge of achieving something that had never been done before? Or was it the thought of this man, so romantic to a modern woman, who stopped his sled, dug in the anchor, took his axe and cut a few branches from the bottom of a fir tree, to light a fire and then cook for the rest of the team? It was certainly appealing, but had I got the guts and tenacity to sled that far? Only time would tell.

Once home, life was very hectic, so it was only a couple of months later that I realised I had heard nothing from Per Thore. I sent an email to see how things were going and to ask if he had thought any more about the trail. What was wrong with me? Nothing happened and I put it all to the back of my mind – other things were taking priority now. Nearly six weeks later, out of the blue, I received an email from him saying 'It's on. I will deal with all the arrangements in Norway, you get the people. We need a maximum of six people. We will go next Easter.' That zap of electricity ran through my body again. Suddenly I had to reprioritise: it looked strongly like I was in charge of organising a team for an Arctic expedition. So taking a deep breath, I called Per Thore on the telephone to discuss the details. He told me his plans for the Nordkapp Expedition and, as he explained more, my imagination became more and more fired up. This was not for charity: this was real exploration.

Per Thore wanted to open up this supposedly impossible trail so that he could take groups keen to dog-sled in more arduous conditions than those of the normal tourist route – which is really just useful to give tourists an idea of how people travel inside the Arctic Circle in the winter, when there is so much snow around. I was so excited, there was a lot to do and I had to start making plans very quickly. Somehow I had to make it work. But I was concentrating hard on other priorities (earning a living, for example) and there were so many other decisions to make. I was in a dilemma; but if I can't see the way to do something I want, I tend to go ahead anyway and believe that somehow it will all work out. Good old Goethe!

Now was that time. At the end of the Charity Challenge, I was the only one to want never to go dog-sledding again. All the others had got off their sleds, said a fond farewell to their dogs and had come into the lodge chattering about how much fun it had been and how they would love to do a trail that was more demanding, where the terrain was harder and the distance longer. They had loved it. They wanted to do a REAL expedition. This was going to be easy, I said to myself: there were eleven other volunteers who were desperate to do something more demanding and I was just about to offer it to them with a leader, Per Thore, they liked and respected. I started to contact those who I thought would be most interested.

Per Thore had said a maximum of six people; that meant we only needed another four, starting with the people who had been with me on the Cancer Research UK challenge. However, what Per Thore had not mentioned was that one of the volunteers who had been on the Cancer Research UK Challenge the week before our group had confirmed that he wanted to join this expedition. If I got nowhere with my companions I could always contact those who had gone on the previous week, I thought. However, the response was good and they wanted to have more details. It was hard to pin Per Thore down about details because at this early stage neither of us really had any idea of what these might be, mainly because we only had the goal and a mere outline idea. The precise details would evolve as the months went by and everything started slotting into place. But I sent my colleagues all that I knew and, to my astonishment, one by one they fell by the wayside. These were the ones who had been looking for more adventurous dog-sledding. I was handing it to them on a plate.

What happened to those people who had come into the Musher's Lodge at the end of the Charity Challenge chattering about how great it had been and wanting more? I was the one who had said 'Done that, been there, never again' and here I was organising something a lot more difficult and dangerous. Next I contacted those I had sailed with on the BT Global Challenge in 2000 who had shown an interest in doing something more taxing but different. By the summer of 2003 we had Per Thore, a guy I didn't know by the name of

David, who had participated in the previous week's Charity Challenge, and me. Unfortunately, Heidi had not been able to raise the sponsorship so had to abandon the challenge.

A couple of years earlier, I had met Cathy at a conference. I can't say that we became firm friends but our paths occasionally crossed and when they did we'd always chat and catch up on what the other had been doing. During the summer of 2003 we bumped into each other again at an event in Kensington, London. It was a very hot and sticky night and I was a little taken aback when, during the conversation, she asked me if I had any plans – not something she usually asked. I explained what Per Thore and I were attempting to do and casually asked whether she was interested in coming along.

Unlike me, she is one of those remarkable women who engage their brains before opening their mouths. As I looked at her, I was positive I could see the cogs in her brain whirring away. Her whole body was still as she contemplated the scenario then the far-away look left her eyes as she focused back on me again and said 'I might well be interested in that, can you let me know some more about it?' As we parted I said 'You never know, we could get some publicity for this.' Little did I realise how such an innocent remark would change my life in the months to come. I emailed all the information I had to her and soon received a response that she would like to join us. So now we were four.

As we drew closer to Christmas, I spoke to Per Thore about the arrangements for the expedition. This got me so excited that I dashed off an email to Cathy and David letting them know what I knew, and by now the main details were virtually set:

> Hallo to you both!
>
> I have just got off the phone from Per Thore and I am so excited. The Nordkapp Route has never been done before. A friend of his has done a bit of it a couple of years ago. So basically we are treading on new ground. It is likely that we will be going up mountains 1,100–1,500 metres (I know that's not too high Cathy but this time we will be running after the dogs in snow!) and down into deep valleys. It will still be 650k but we will have eight dogs each – I must be stark raving mad to do this! There are dangers doing something like this – dogs getting hurt, we might and the sled might break.
>
> Per Thore has built some good strong sleds for us but we will have to carry all of our gear. There will be one drop point where we will be able to pick up more food (for us and the dogs) as well as fuel and be able to mend sleds if necessary. Because of the time of year

we may turn a day around and sled by the full moon (!) through one night. We will be up near where the Sámi people look after the reindeer and there are lots of loose reindeer around so we may come across a herd of 10,000 which means that we will just have to wait for them to cross – holding firmly onto the dogs.

We will drive round Finnmark's biggest mountain! Half the time we will camp. Cathy, Per Thore says we are to decide whether we have one five-man tent and all get in it or he will bring two smaller tents – one for the girls and one for the boys! Not sure how you guys are thinking of going but I think we should meet in Oslo and fly to Tromsø together. Per Thore will pick us up and take us to our tent, we will sort everything out pack the sleds and set off the next day.

Once we get to Nordkapp we will take the coastal steamer back – it will go along the coast of Norway past all the fjords and fishing villages (better than being in a car). We also need to let Per Thore know what size feet, hands and bodies we have. He will let us have a kit list. He is away now until Christmas – only just got him! So all I can say is that this sounds extremely exciting – Per Thore has always wanted to do this as well so it will be new to all of us.

If you have any questions let me know and I will find out the answers. Might be an idea to let me know whether you intend to come to the UK and then fly to Oslo but I will be checking out flights so I think before we book we should liaise. Per Thore thinks we should book just after Christmas but I think for convenience and fun we should at least meet in Oslo if not before and fly into Tromsø together! Wow, I can't wait – now this is an incentive for the training!

All the best folks – hope that helps.

I carried on looking for some more people to join us but I was happy that we had four stalwarts, so the expedition was definitely on. In the autumn, I met up with Cathy to discuss the expedition and to show her the route that Per Thore had set out for us, in the hope that we could find a way through. Towards the end of the year, I heard from her again and was a little taken back at first. She had looked at what we were planning to do and wanted to use this expedition as a way of getting away from her usual expeditions on mountains. She had written as such in her CV. Cathy was keen to get the expedition sponsored, which I think was usual for her (my bank manager and

I certainly had nothing against that) and to use a publicist to raise awareness of her as well as that of the expedition. She also wanted to produce a website. Cathy already knew that I intended to write a book about our adventures along the way – but a publicist?

This all came as a shock as I have always been in the habit of paying my own way on any expedition (which probably explains my financial situation at the time) and the publicity that I have acquired has been from the local TV, radio and newspapers. It was quite a departure for me and one with which I was not entirely comfortable. Whenever I feel challenged like this, where I used to jump in with 'Oh no I don't think we should do that', I now I tend to wait quietly and watch to see what it may involve. If it appears to be do-able then I go along with it to see how it develops. For the moment then, it was 'watch and wait time' as I really did not know exactly what this would involve. However, I had to be honest with Cathy and say to her that I really could not afford to pay for a publicist. She very rapidly produced two names – one publicist and one for sponsorship. We agreed that she would interview the publicist and I would interview the guy for sponsorship. Cathy's interview went well. However, when I spoke to the guy I was to interview, I felt very wary; but we organised a convenient time to meet and he was to call me to suggest a mutually convenient venue.

I was even more wary when, having spoken to him twice to try to ascertain the venue, we arrived at the morning of our 10 a.m. meeting and I still did not know where we were meeting. He lived south of London and I was in Oxford: it couldn't be that difficult to organise. I called that morning, it sounded as though I had woken him. Some rapid thinking was done on his part and the name of a hotel by Heathrow Airport was put forward. This was going to be very tight time-wise for me. It was nearly Christmas and the expedition was to start at Easter. Time was definitely of the essence if a sponsor was to reap the rewards of the expedition and the efforts made by our publicist, Alex Foley.

He confirmed that he knew lots of people in the city and didn't think that getting sponsorship would be a problem as he was used to dealing with much larger figures (we only wanted to cover our costs and get some money for charity). He then asked me whether I had any ideas for sponsorship and he would get onto it right away. Surely we were paying him to come up with the ideas?

I telephoned Cathy in Andorra and relayed my feelings; but as she rightly said, trying to raise sponsorship is very difficult and we didn't have any other options. As Alex and Cathy were keen to use him, I had no choice but to go along with it against my better judgement. I was a novice at this aspect of expeditions and they were the experts, so I didn't feel I could make too much of an issue about it. I had voiced my concerns. Now we just had to hope that he would prove me wrong.

Christmas came and went, my children came home for the festivities. Nicola had left home to start her job in November and Simon would be off to start his new job in the New Year.

January started what were to be a crazy five months. Early on Cathy and I met up prior to our meeting with Alex to discuss how we wanted to proceed. Our man for sponsorship sent his apologies – not the most auspicious of starts. After the meeting we were joined by a journalist and continued our discussions over lunch. There then started a round of interviews on radio, television and with newspapers to let as many people as possible know about the expedition.

Both Cathy and I had always taken lots of photos of whatever we were doing and this would be no exception. In fact, Cathy brought up the idea of making a documentary. At first the idea was that we would do all the filming ourselves. Then Cathy suggested that maybe we could get someone to film it for us. A number of discussions took place with various film companies to find a perfect fit. By luck I met someone who had worked with the MD of a television company who had already made documentaries of this type before. We decided that, if we could, we would have a fifth member of the team, there primarily to film the expedition. Whoever it was would have to sled and film at the same time. Not a particularly easy exercise on the terrain we were going to encounter. It was now even more imperative to get the sponsorship in order to cover our costs, which seemed to be mounting. But that side was not working well.

Cathy was the 'techie' of the team and built a fantastic website for us, containing all the relevant details the sponsors or the public could want to know about the expedition. In the top-left-hand corner she had inserted the head of a husky with a quote underneath, but as these quotes were the same on each page I provided some alternatives to make it more fun and varied. On the Home page the caption was 'You want me to go where? Who are these women, anyway?' On the Project page it was: 'You want me to do what? Oh boy, this could be interesting!' When it came to describing the team the caption was 'A sailor and a mountaineer! Well, at least there's one of us who knows what they're doing.' On the page listing the facts about dog-sleds it read 'OK, so we come first – now you're getting the idea' and on the Contact page the caption was 'Hey, talk to me – I can tell you the real facts.' A good deal of work had gone into ensuring that our CVs were correct and choosing the right photographs to put up on the website to give a flavour of what we were about to embark on. These photographs came mainly from my visit to Sweden the previous year for the Charity Challenge. I also had to make sure that I had all the right facts about the dogs so these could be included. We received some excellent feedback from it but what we really hoped was that it would enthuse someone enough to sponsor the expedition.

By the end of January, we had our first snowfall of the winter and, unfortunately, our man for sponsorship succumbed to the slippery surfaces, breaking his collarbone in the process. This was bad news all round, painful both for him and for us. We were paying a publicist to raise awareness of the expedition in order to get sponsorship and the team member who was to utilise this was incapacitated at a crucial time. Alex agreed to talk to him and it transpired that the break was very bad and that the operation would have to be repeated. It was fairly obvious that even with the best technology in the world this team member was not in any position to fulfil his part of our campaign, so an alternative strategy had to be instituted.

We asked for a comprehensive list of everyone he had approached, their contact details and responses. I have to say that, when we eventually received this spreadsheet, we were somewhat aghast to find it contained only eleven names after more than a month of work, some of which we had provided. The contact details were incomplete and it looked strongly as if we were really still at square one. I can't say that I was unhappy that he was now out of the picture; but if we were to get the sponsorship then something had to be done and done quickly, otherwise we would be paying all the costs ourselves. With just about two months left before we departed the job fell onto my shoulders. This was going to be a very steep learning curve for me. Although those I spoke to were enthusiastic, it was the end of the financial year and they had run out of money. We would have to pay our own way.

About this time I received an email from Per Thore

Hi Rona

The web site looks nice. We will put our own website out on the net in the middle of February. I will give you the address then. Right now it's just too few hours in the day; it should have been 72 instead of 24. I'm just finished with the last sled for the expedition (four of them) + I have made 15 sleds for the ATD trips in March. There is a lot to organize to get those trips running.

I had a meeting with my friend, Tom Frode Johansen, who has done part of this route before, and we were planning on how far we shall drive every day – where is a good place to put up the tents – how much dog food we need etc. are going well. There will be a lot of weight on the sleds – we need for example 20 kilo of meat for the dogs every day + dry food. But that's the easy things to find out. What takes time to put together is all the bits and pieces that we need to repair the sleds on the trail. All the camp equipment is OK. I still had to order the tents and the sled bags. I haven't been able to get somebody to sponsor us Gore-Tex dresses, but I will try to talk to a company called Fjellreven.

I knew exactly how Per Thore felt; there really were not enough hours in the day for either of us. I had kept Per Thore informed of all the publicity that we were raising for the Expedition. A week later, I received another email from Per Thore:

Hi Rona/Cathy

Looks like we are going to be famous on our 'little' dogsled trip. I have used the weekend to pack most of the dog food for the expedition + I have been training the dogs quite hard. Yesterday I did drive a 12-dog team on a 35-kilometre trip, it was a fast one... I only used 1.5 hours on it.

But we won't be going that fast because of the weight of the sleds. Right now it looks like that we will have a depot in Kautokeino. It will mostly be dog food in the depot. I will try to rent a cabin from the Norwegian Government some kilometres from Kautokeino – that could be the only time on those 10 days we will be in a house. We will stay in tent, and we will have two of them. The tents are Expeditions tents, similar to those that are used on North Pole Expeditions.

On the trip we will change on feeding the dogs – making dinner etc. That brings me over to an important question – are any of you vegetarians????

So we had 10 days to do over 500 kilometres. We would also have to stop for a couple of days to let the dogs rest because they would be pulling very heavy sleds – little did I know just how heavy they would be. It was exciting to hear of all these arrangements, it made the whole expedition seem so much more real. All I could see from my side at this time was the lack of sponsorship, the need to attain the right level of fitness along with all the other things that I needed to arrange – let alone building my own business.

Sometimes when things are not going as well as you'd like, everything seems to constrain and work against you. Towards the end of February, still reeling from the sponsorship issue, I was up early in order to catch the coach into London for a meeting. The coach was sitting there as I drove into the car park and I was only five metres from the stop when it left – frustration! It was very early in the morning and it was very cold waiting for the next coach. It crossed my mind – do I really need to go to the Arctic? Isn't Britain cold enough? I don't think we had had a winter as cold as this for a long time. But Cathy was in England for two weeks and we needed to make the most of it. We met up with Sean, a photographer we'd been recommended, near Piccadilly to discuss the expedition and how it would be filmed and to see whether we might get on with him. I'd not seen this much of Cathy before but so far we seemed to be getting along and had the same mindset on most aspects of the expedition. We'd spent the last two days together, being interviewed by Bloomberg TV and then on to Boisdale to prepare for a talk to the Explorers' Club. However, this was the evening we were to have our first experience of not communicating properly.

Having discussed who would speak first and decided on Cathy, we omitted to convey the result to Alex, who had organised the event. Suddenly Alex got up, introduced us and asked me to talk first. Despite this, the audience seemed to enjoy what we said and we eventually left just before midnight, racing to the Underground before it closed. It was manic but we both finally arrived home – Cathy was staying with her Aunt in Wimbledon and I had to get back to Oxford.

After only a few hours' sleep, I was back on the coach returning to London again when my mobile rang. It was Sean. We had got on well and he was as excited as we were about the expedition; but now he was saying that he was really sorry, he had to call it a day. He would not be able to come with us either to Andorra for our training weekend nor on the expedition as he'd been unable to sell the documentary. It appears that interest in adventure films was flagging. Other people wanted him to do paid work and he had to give them an answer. It was too risky to participate in the expedition in the hope of being able to sell the film on our return.

I was devastated. We talked for ages trying to think of a way that we could pay for him to come with us but nothing came to mind. Eventually, I had to concede that he was right. He was so nice and it would have been good to have had him along with us.

Cathy was also disappointed when I told her of Sean's decision. We would have to think of someone else and quickly. By now we were at LBC waiting to be interviewed by Sandi Toksvig, but I think the news had affected us. At Bloomberg we had managed to mention sponsorship and the webpage but this time we didn't – in fact I must own up to my mind wandering off to the autocue at one point. It was fascinating. I just hope I answered the question I had been asked correctly! After we had finished, Sandi asked if there was anything that they could do for us and she kindly agreed to mention our website and that we were looking for sponsorship.

Trying to fit everything in was a nightmare. I really needed to become fit for this expedition as both Cathy and Per Thore were in their thirties and I was not! So a session at the gym was required. In fact, several sessions were required.

For the Charity Challenge the previous year I had done some training to get my upper body fit, only to find out on the route that I really needed strong legs as the sleds were light but I needed to run up mountains. However, the only training option Cancer Research UK offered was walking in the Derbyshire and Yorkshire Dales with Gideon of Walkwise. I had no idea that the temperature dropped so low in the Dales. Whilst it was very enjoyable, it was not really comprehensive enough for dog-sledding. So for this expedition I decided not to get caught out and to concentrate on getting my legs as fit as possible. Hmmm, I hadn't quite got the whole picture in my mind.

In late February, I spoke to Per Thore on the telephone. He said that the temperature on a good day would be 0°C during the day and that it would go down to -20°C or -30°C at night. He had been talking to a friend near to where we would have a food drop and the temperature there was -45°C – which was normal! However, Per Thore did say that the first day would be very hard as the dogs would be raring to go. I knew exactly what he meant by that – pictures of us setting off on the Charity Challenge out of the woods came flashing back into my mind.

Per Thore also said that if Sean, the photographer, had been coming he wouldn't have been able to film and dog-sled up the really tricky first part of the route. Instead, he would have had to go up the mountain on a snowmobile on the first day and film from the top, 1,000 metres up. In fact, the experienced mushers of Norway thought that, as our sleds were so heavy, this was where they were most likely to break, going up the mountain through the forest on the very first day. Meanwhile, Per Thore's wife, Hege, would have taken the sled up the mountain for Sean and then gone back down on the snowmobile. But as, unfortunately, Sean was now not coming, Per Thore decided to ask his friend, Ryno, to film the first day for us. He was really looking forward to this expedition as it would be better when there were only a few people. He also mentioned that he thought I was fit! Oh dear, that meant more sessions in the gym to live up to his expectations.

Then came the bad news. David telephoned to say that he would be dropping out. He had had to make the choice between a family holiday in Canada and the dog-sledding expedition. When he heard that Cathy wanted to make a documentary, he chose Canada. He wanted to be able to dog-sled without having to stop every so often to film. I was really disappointed that he would not be coming as I knew from Per Thore that he had been very keen and I thought I understood about the filming. When we filmed on the round-the-world yacht race we had kept moving! Little did I realise what an intrusion filming can be to an expedition like this.

Cathy arrived at my house the following Thursday and we did some work on the expedition before having an early night. We were to be up at four the next morning to catch a flight from Luton to Andorra for our training weekend. For Cathy this was going home; for me it was a new adventure. This weekend would be our only opportunity to check that all the communication and camera equipment was working and to test out our skills with dog-sleds. It would be a very effective training as the temperature in Andorra was -11°C. Why is it that when you are tired and have to be up early, for some reason you wake up about two hours before the alarm goes off? Then your mind starts racing so you cannot get back to sleep. I could think of all the things I needed to do in the next few days but there was no time. It was just five weeks until we were to head off to the last wilderness in Europe.

However, the real question was how would Cathy and I get on when seeing so much of each other? Would the relationship build into a friendship or disintegrate? Also, how would we get on when we were exhausted, cold and the dogs needed to be fed?

Little did I realise how appropriate my apprehensions would turn out to be.

CHAPTER 2

Training in Andorra

It seemed no time at all until the alarm finally went off and, after a swift breakfast, we had packed the car and set off in thick fog. It only started to clear as we climbed through a cutting towards the Berkshire border. Travelling the other way the previous evening, as the coach drove through this cutting, out of sight of motorists and lorry drivers, but there in the shady depths of the beech wood at the top of the cutting, were a group of deer – male and female, stationary, listening, ready to run but undisturbed by the sound of the nearby motorway traffic. But yesterday was a different world. We dropped the hire car off at the airport and headed for the check-in desk.

Soon we had taken off on a very bumpy ride until we were high above the clouds. This training weekend would show us exactly what was still required of us in the way of fitness and expertise at photography, and would also be a chance to take some video footage of us in action – publicity for the television companies back in the UK. Cathy had never dog-sled before but had eventually managed to find a man who had husky dogs and sleds in Andorra, so we were hoping to practise in a country where there was plenty of snow. We had alerted the media and prospective sponsors that we were going away for training; the media wanted footage for news items and we were hoping that this would also encourage the prospective sponsors to take the plunge. Suddenly, through the window, I saw the Pyrenees gleaming white in the sun – a far cry from the fog we had left in the UK. Having landed and collected the baggage, we headed for the coffee shop as it was nearly four hours until the coach would leave to take us to Cathy's house. Refreshed and nourished we found the right coach for Andorra and soon we were off on the four-hour journey to Cathy's home.

This weekend we were also going to review the situation regarding the publicist and the expedition. We agreed that it appeared to be working well and Cathy confirmed she would like to continue using Alex until about three weeks after the expedition. Now I was really in a dilemma. A number of journalists had commented that mine was the story, as I had been a stay-at-home Mum before taking on a life of adventure whereas Cathy had climbed mountains all her life. Living in Andorra, Cathy was not always available for interviews, photo shoots and so on. Of course, if Cathy's profile was being raised so was mine; but at the moment, Cathy was footing the bill. There was nothing for it. I had to pay my way for my own peace of mind. Taking a deep breath, I told Cathy that I would repay my share somehow or other, but couldn't do so at the moment. She was happy to accept that at some point, in the not too distant future, she would get her money. We were really quite a good foil for each other: I am all for the power of positive thinking and Cathy is somewhat sceptical, preferring to make contingency plans. My resolve now was to focus on the sponsorship and hers to get a loan from a prospective sponsor, which would be paid back over the long term in return for giving the sponsor publicity. This road to sponsorship was certainly a hard one but, hopefully, would soon pay dividends.

As the coach trundled along, the hills became steeper and the mountains grew closer and closer together, spectacular views coming with each turn of the road. It was magical for me. I simply love mountains and am mesmerised by water; for Cathy, who had seen it all so many times before, it was a chance to catch up on some much needed sleep. Nearly missing our stop, we grabbed our cases, got off the bus and walked up a higgledy-piggledy steep cobbled path to Cathy's house. There was no level ground – no wonder she was so fit. Dumping our cases, we did a tour of the village with its breath-taking views. Whilst Cathy walked unfalteringly, I was slipping and sliding on patches of ice. I could see Alex back in the UK issuing a press release with the headline 'Nordkapp Expedition cancelled as organiser injured on small patch of ice'. Not the most glorious of endings to any expedition, to end before it had even begun.

Cathy spent some time trying to contact the man whose dogs we would be using for our training but to no avail. It transpired that he was away at weekends and the woman who usually took over was on a leadership course. Trying to find another contact number for him, Cathy put his name into her computer and came up with a site that told of him dog-sledding across Patagonia with an all-man team. Cathy and I just looked at each other. Could this be our next expedition together – the first women to... I touched her arm and said 'Let's get this one under our belts first'.

The time came for us to do some training but no-one seemed to speak English and Cathy only had elementary Spanish. Eventually we managed to organise for dogs, sleds and David, their owner, to be available for some training the next day. Cathy had been a media student so in preparation she gave me lessons on how to take a good photograph. These were to be used on the website to encourage sponsors.

Photo 1 – Training in Andorra (see page 115)

When we arrived, David had already taken the dogs for two runs up and down the trail to get rid of some of their energy before I was to take control of the sled. After all, he had no idea what my level of expertise at dog-sledding was. As we set off, I was so scared and all my old insecurities came flooding to the fore – would I fall off in front of the small crowd of onlookers who were curious to know what was going on? My legs were shaking like a jelly as we began the trail but it was great. My fears as usual were unfounded: I was fitter than I thought.

Back at the house, we reviewed the results of our morning's work. I hadn't got the filming quite right but then I was a novice. I was to take the tape back to the UK to distribute to the various interested television stations. We were still hoping to get sponsorship for some of the filming equipment. The next morning I would be on the 4.30 a.m. bus to the airport. However, I wanted to re-film everything we had done, this time with me standing up straight so that I could say 'Hey look everyone, I'm nearly as tall as Cathy, I don't really come up to her knees!' I slept so soundly that night that I was totally disorientated when the alarm went off – I thought I was back in my own bed in Oxford. There was a full moon and it was bitterly cold. The bus arrived and, bidding Cathy goodbye, off I went. There was only one other person on board.

The more time Cathy and I spent together, the more we got to know each other and luckily, at that moment, the better we got on. On the trail we would only really be together in a small tent at the end of the day when we were tired, hungry and still with lots of work to do (updating the website, writing notes for this book, checking photographs); so it was helpful to understand what each other was like. It was now clear that I am a dreamer and optimist whilst Cathy is more sceptical and realistic. Definitely a good foil for each other!

The bus was far too cold to allow any sleep and I would have a long wait once I got to Barcelona until my flight. I decided to explore and visited the local department store. Big, huge mistake! You should never go into a decent department store when you have just come down from the mountains early in the morning and are dressed in hiking boots, thick socks, fleece, bum-bag and quilt-lined hiking jacket. Especially if you have just spent nearly three hours on the top of an open-deck tourist bus being blown to pieces. Not only do the assistants look at you as if you are an alien but so do the shoppers. Resist the temptation, as not only will you be classed as an outcast but you can be sure that sooner or later you will pass a full-length mirror and the impression you have of yourself will come crashing to the ground as you catch a glimpse of your reflection amidst the smartly dressed shoppers. My advice is leave the store by the quickest exit and catch the bus to the airport where you will be amongst a motley selection of dressers and you will blend in. Banish the memory of that reflection and focus your mind on what you have been doing for the past two days – and refrain from any use of a mirror until you have showered and dressed yourself again in a decent outfit.

I was exhausted by the time I eventually arrived home. It had been a great morale booster but there was no time to lose. The video needed to be copied and distributed, the photographs developed and sent to both the publicist and Cathy. There was still the question of sponsorship looming over me: Cathy wanted enough to cover our costs otherwise it would have to come out of our pockets and mine weren't exactly full at that moment. We only needed £25,000 but we had left it late and our timing was wrong. Cathy was going to contact the one hope that she had whilst I would continue to approach companies that, I hoped, would welcome the opportunity to raise their profiles. Those I approached confirmed they would have loved to be doing the expedition, they wished us luck, they would follow us... and lovely as that was, all I could think of was GIVE US THE MONEY! It was soul destroying and deeply depressing.

Taking another look at the website, I realised that I had not provided very many 'Diary notes'. There was one from Cathy saying that all the preparations had been made. NO they hadn't – we still did not have any sponsorship. It's strange how suddenly everything can change and I was getting through to people who had proved elusive; not only that but one of them recommended that I contact her counterpart in a competitor company as they might be able to help. So dutifully I called and got the most positive response to date. At the same time, our guy for sponsorships suddenly reappeared with a hot lead. One of the television companies suddenly got excited about the expedition and wanted to film me in the gym (hmmm) and then do a live interview the next day. Was this déjà vu? Central Television had wanted to film me packing my rucksack when I was embarking on the Charity Challenge. However, we decided that this was not really good television as all the interesting equipment was already in Sweden. I sent the following email copying it to Cathy to keep her in the loop:

Anna,

I have just received directions to Jonathan's office – we meet at 4 p.m. next Thursday.

As to Sky I have spoken with Sam and they are going to film me in the gym on Friday (I can't wait! – yes Cathy I am sitting upright as I write!) and then I shall go into the Studio Saturday morning. The idea is that Sam will put together photos/film etc. (she thinks the footage from Andorra is great – especially where I am filming the snow and our knees Cathy!) and I will talk about how we met and what is going to happen. There's some very clever timing going on here as I am at a Literary Festival most of the weekend.

As to sponsors, the same is happening to me – Cathy I have tried Nick and left a voicemail – he is at an exhibition today.

Speak soon

Rona

The response from Cathy came winging back!

Dear Rona

The Sky interview sounds cool. Stomach in, shoulders back, boobs out, and remember to glow, not sweat!

If you get the chance, ask Sam for some tips from the footage – what sort of stuff would they like to see? What did they like from Andorra, what would they like that we didn't provide?

I think we may well be doing our own filming. I have found a source of high-power expedition camera batteries in the USA, and will be geared up for us to do it ourselves.

Cathy

I raced around to collect videos and DVDs before getting to the gym just in time to meet the television company. But 2 p.m. came and went; so did 2.15 and 2.25. I waited and waited. Eventually I asked for a telephone directory and called the News Desk only to be told that the film crew were not coming and 'hadn't I been told?' Needless to say, the alleged Islamic attack on Madrid in which a bomb exploded on a train took precedence. There were profuse apologies that no-one had called me to cancel. Home I went, but a call came through later to confirm that Sky wanted the live interview the following morning. Timing was tight as the interview was to go out at 9.45 a.m. and I had to get to North Oxfordshire to talk at a Literary Festival at 11.30 a.m.

The next morning the van was late turning up. They called me only to find that they were behind a parked bakery van on the wrong side of the bollards that made my road a cul-de-sac. I guided them round to my house. Everything was set up for the interview to take place in the street. However, not having used this particular van before, there were a few technical problems; but as each arose it was dealt with. The schedule deadline drew closer and we miked up but the connecting wire did not work. It was changed and I spoke to the studio in London as a test. We were right on time and just about to 'go' when the call came through that, although we were beaming pictures to the satellite on the studio roof, they had technical problems at their end and could not download them into the studio so the interview was off. It was all so frustrating.

I sent an email to Cathy:

Hi Cathy,

So I waited at the gym – standing very erect! At 2.30 I called Sky – they had decided that the Spanish bomb was more important, scrubbed me, but had not told me! (Not surprising really.) Apparently they will do a live interview here with a cable van outside – should be interesting – or we may be outside!

Spoke with Sam she was the one to organise the interview – she had only scanned the video very quickly. So in response to your questions about filming she said – didn't see anyone sled (I explained the shot and colour – me in red jacket); more talking between ourselves (we can do that on the trail); feelings, tearful moments – talking to the video; making tea, what eating; set camera up – snow, walk from left through shot to right or right through shot to left.

In other words, you have it totally right but when we are on the trail we need to do more of the up close and personal saying how we feel to each other and alone and general chat (slightly staged I would have thought) and us just surviving the cold, the food, feeding the dogs. I would have thought not too much is required of us sledding. Probably, just on the first day and some on the flat but more when we stop than when we are going along. Unless of course something happens – reindeer, someone falls off, meet animal etc.

Rona

Cathy's response was:

Dear Rona

Such is life. Everything was going to be secondary to the bombing. Imagine how we felt leaving for our 2003 expedition just as the Iraq war started. No chance of publicity.

Thanks for the video stuff. I am keen to use this trip to learn all I can about filming in such conditions.

Cathy

I managed to send Cathy a 'diary note' for the website:

28 March

Well, it's been a kaleidoscope of emotions as we come to the run up to the start of this expedition. Cathy and I agreed that we had achieved a considerable amount on our training weekend and I came back to England refreshed and ready to really go for the sponsorship and follow up all the leads I could possibly find.

Interspersed with the sponsorship issue I had meetings and talks to deal with as this was my career and I could not put it completely on hold. There were telephone calls to Per Thore's wife as last minute arrangements were made so that we could organise the flights. I left this to Cathy as it had defeated me and, like the organised lady she is, it was soon dealt with.

I also had my speaking career to deal with which entailed going to Liverpool and Manchester. It is certainly good that Cathy and Per Thore are with me on the expedition as I managed to get lost four times, once in Liverpool and three times in Manchester. This trip meant that the telephone calls had to wait until the following Monday when they all started off again. It is soul destroying to sit on the telephone day after day contacting companies, following up contacts and getting rejected time and time again. But we still have two weeks until we leave so there's still time to find a sponsor.

That week was one of those messy ones where you seem to be thwarted no matter what you do. It was not helped by the fact that something I had eaten or drunk did not agree with me. I think it was fizzy water. It would be so nice to say that I had been trying some new exotic recipe and some obscure ingredient had caused the problem but no, it was fizzy water.

On 30 March just eight days before we left for Norway we had a breakthrough. I emailed Cathy with the following:

Eureka! We have our first sponsorship cheque. It is a light at the end of a very long tunnel. Today, quite unsolicited I received a cheque for £25 it felt sooo good. We only have nine days and £24,975 to go. I spoke to one company today who said they may well be able to give us our passage back from Nordkapp on the steamer as they own the steamer. He will let me know!

A few days later, we received a cheque for £1,000. It just shows that you should never give up as you never know what could be around the corner. It reminded me of the Cancer Research UK Charity Challenge the year before when I had struggled to raise the money – but then I'd discovered out of the blue that National Grid, the company that I was working for, had a policy of matching the total if it was for charity and came to my rescue at the final hour. Suddenly all was well, everything felt great – just how fickle can you be?

CHAPTER 3

Now the Fun Begins

How can I say this? I was feeling sick. It was just three days until we were to leave and I was experiencing pains in my stomach and had nearly been physically sick several times already. We had a conference call that morning at 10 a.m. GMT between Cathy, Alex and me, to finalise arrangements; by the time I got off the telephone I felt even worse. I managed to eat some lunch, felt a little better and went to meet up with some friends – a pleasant interlude in all the hurry and flurry of the preparations. But it was all to get a lot worse. I arrived home and deteriorated rapidly. In fact, I spent the evening running upstairs to the bathroom. The next day I had an important meeting followed by a talk to give at a venue in Wales. I really should have been practising for it but I could only sit. To add to my malaise, I was beginning to worry again as to whether I could cope with this challenge. I had had a niggling concern for several weeks now, simply because Per Thore and Cathy were in their 30s and I was not. All my old insecurities reared their ugly heads again and laughed at me: they seemed to have a look which said 'Really woman, act your age – who do you think you are? You really think you're up to this when you were so relieved to get off the sled last March after a much tamer challenge.'

However, these anxieties were there at the forefront of my mind and no matter how much I tried, I just could not push them away. They had been simmering under the surface for weeks now. Was I being silly? Should I listen to the sceptics and get a 'normal' job, go back to what I know I can earn a living at, go back to the safe and familiar? But try as I might to get myself to believe that I could do that, there was always a voice saying 'But you won't be happy, you'll be secure but you'll never settle.' I spent the evening sitting quietly on the settee (when I could) drinking one of my sports drinks, the same one that I had offered to help revive Sue in March the year before on the Charity Challenge after she had been very ill at the end of the trail. Gradually, I could feel some strength return. I went to bed literally praying that I would make a quick recovery.

The next day I went to see my bank manager who knew that we were looking for sponsorship. Now I had to tell her that 48 hours before we were to leave the UK we had the princely sum of £1,025 – not quite the £25,000 we were looking for – and so would have to pay virtually all of the costs ourselves. I also needed to discuss my future plans with her. The expedition may have been imminent but there was a life after sledding and I had bills to pay; with virtually no sponsorship there would be a lot more. As ever, she was receptive and appeared pleased and positive with the direction of my career. As to my future plans, I was to call her on my return and we would work something out. Was that ominous? I hoped not.

Once I was home, it was a case of packing the car and heading west to Wales. Strangely, my navigational skills were working overtime and I arrived where and when I should. I rewarded myself with a smiley face. As I left my last port of call, I had a voicemail from Cathy – there was a crisis, would I call as soon as I got home. The car ate up the miles and just after 11 p.m. I called. For Cathy in Andorra it was midnight, she wasn't packed and the bus to Barcelona was the same one that I had caught at 4.30 a.m. on the training weekend. When she answered the phone, she sounded understandably just a little stressed. The next few minutes revealed why. Cathy had bought some expensive technical equipment for our expedition so that we would be able to call in to various radio stations as well as update our website as we travelled. However, there was one glaring omission. The equipment required a large number of specialised batteries. It was too late to order them on the web for delivery to me and anyway the postmen were on strike in Oxford. There was only one answer – either, on her arrival in the UK, Cathy would have to go into London to search for them or I had to do some research and find them near me. I jumped onto the web and searched. After what seemed like ages, but was actually only about 30 minutes, I had two places in Kent and one in Putney.

Despite there being some telephone numbers on the web pages, there were no people at the end of the line. Out came the Yellow Pages and my finger started walking. Time and time again the response was negative. Was this the sponsorship pattern all over again? I couldn't leave it to Cathy to get them. She had been up all night and travelling for eight hours to get to England. I carried on and eventually an advertisement by T4 Cameras Ltd. based in Witney caught my eye. I made my enquiry with the precise details of the battery and to my amazement the guy said 'Yes, we have those.' 'Really?' 'Yes.' 'Do you have a lot?' 'About 14 packs, each with two batteries.' 'Can you put them aside for me please?' 'How many do you want?' 'All of them – I need

30 to 40 in total.' Success. I called another shop which was in Banbury and yes, I was on a roll, they had three packets. That gave me 34 – that was good enough at this late stage.

I was just about to jump into the car when the telephone rang. The local paper was sending a photographer and he would be with me at noon. It was now 11.30 a.m. Cathy's plane landed at 12.15 p.m. and, if she was lucky with the buses, I envisaged she might be in Oxford before 3.00 p.m. The very least I could do was to be there to pick her up when she arrived. The paper had called earlier in the day and I had tried to arrange the photographer for about half four and the interview nearer that time so that Cathy could be in both, but it wasn't possible. The journalist was very amenable when I told her of our crisis and got the photographer to turn up earlier. We took several shots in the garden then I bade him farewell and high-tailed off to Witney. T4 Cameras came up trumps. They had found an extra three packs – we would have our 40. He asked why we wanted all these batteries so I told him about the expedition we were just about to start. He was extremely helpful and also gave me a discount for quantity, so I thanked him and promised they would get a mention in the book. He took a note of our website and said he would follow us. I asked another customer in the shop the quickest way to get to Banbury and hurried off.

The Banbury shop was more difficult to locate but soon I was heading home having received a message from Cathy: she would be arriving at 4.50 p.m. That was somewhat disappointing as I had hoped we would have a little more time, but having landed and heard that I had located the batteries, she had decided to take the easy option of a bus from Luton to Oxford and not chase round the country trying to save time. I certainly couldn't blame her, the previous 60 hours must have been very frustrating. Having heard that the new equipment had arrived in Andorra she had organised that it would be delivered early Monday morning. That hadn't happened, so Tuesday saw her driving the length and breadth of the country (yes, Andorra is only relatively small as countries go but it still takes time – the roads are windy and certainly not fast) to find out where the courier was. Eventually she found the depot at the end of a maze of streets. The doors were open but no-one was home. Not one to be defeated, Cathy found her parcel for herself and left. Time was of the essence and we needed to know (well, Cathy did at least) how to work the equipment and upload or download everything so that the website could be a running record of our journey.

Finally, the coach from Luton arrived and, having gathered Cathy and her belongings, I took her home and we set about the final preparations. Cathy homed in on the equipment and I sent my last emails. Then it was a photo session of Cathy and the kit.

Photo 2 — How does this go?

Now, Cathy had given me lessons on our training weekend about how to take a good photo. I had done well but this new one on how to make technical equipment look sexy – even with Cathy in the photo – was defeating me. Also there was still more shopping to do – we needed to visit my local supermarket for zip-lock bags to pack equipment and treats for on the trail and, having been up all the previous night, Cathy was beginning to fight a losing battle. Once everything was bagged, Cathy repacked her bag and headed to bed for a decent few hours' sleep.

Me? Well I still had to finish sending some emails, iron some clothes and then start my packing! Suddenly, a shout came from upstairs 'Have you booked the taxi?' 'Just doing it,' I replied as I dashed for the telephone directory. We sent our last despatch from the UK to the publicist:

> Finally the day has arrived – we're leaving behind the city, the noise
> and the stress and heading out to snow, sleds and silence plus 26
> howling huskies!

What time did I finally make it to bed? 1.20 a.m. The alarm rang at five and we were up and ready when the taxi arrived to take us to the bus station to catch the coach to Heathrow. Once we had checked in and relieved ourselves of our luggage we made our way to the departure lounge. This was very different from last year when I raised money for Cancer Research: when I had arrived at the airport there was a crowd of us meeting at the check-in desks with Claire Bewell (the Cancer Research UK representative) to greet us and ensure everyone was there, give us our tickets and see that our bags were checked in. We then spent the time in the departure lounge getting to know each other and talking nineteen to the dozen.

This was a very different start to our expedition: just the two of us and no exciting chatter or making new friends. Very shortly Simon, my son, appeared. It was lovely to see him and I really appreciated his support and the effort he put in to ensure that someone was there to wish us luck and send us on our way. He, too, had been up at the crack of dawn to travel from south-east London to see us off. We sat drinking coffee and chatting until Simon had to leave to get to work. Cathy and I had some shopping to do, including presents for Per Thore and his wife as we would be staying with them for a couple days before the start of the expedition. I had already bought Easter eggs for the children. So we said our farewells to Simon and headed towards the departure gate. We thought the flight might well be delayed because of the weather but, luckily, we did not have to wait too long. It was a clear day and I had a window seat. Soon the patchwork of Great Britain was thousands of feet below us as the pilot turned the aircraft towards the North Sea.

All the time we were in the air Cathy was updating the website and I was writing my journal. After flying over the North Sea for some considerable time suddenly, below us, were a number of islands glimpsed through the clouds. This was the coast of Norway. It was astonishing, the islands became more numerous, growing larger and then smaller, becoming more scattered then gradually starting to join up again as we flew over our first fjord. In my mind's eye I could see the flooded mountain range below sea level. As I went back to writing my journal, we reached the mainland. Almost immediately we were above a very urban industrialised area with quarries, then across another fjord, and I could see towns interspersed with pine forests in which nestled frozen lakes. What an incredible country Norway was. It was an aeronautical geography lesson. But this was only the beginning: much more was to come.

We had left a spring-like England bathed in sunshine but here, as I strained my neck to look down through the window, were more and more patches of snow and frozen lakes to be seen. It reminded me of flying into Kiruna, last year, only this time we would be going much further north. I still try to get the window seat whenever I fly – it gives an opportunity to get a better understanding of the countries you are flying above.

Oslo Airport was very different from Heathrow, being tidy and efficiently laid out, but everywhere was brown and grey. The brown was the newly exposed earth after its winter hibernation and the grey the steel of the buildings. The terminal building was architecturally beautiful – true Scandinavian style, cool, clear and elegantly made of wood, steel and marble.

We collected our bags and looked for the coffee shop. (Can you see a pattern here?) Once the appropriate beverages had been procured, we eventually returned to our chores. We were so engrossed, neither of us noticed the time slowly ticking away until suddenly I realised that Cathy had gone to change her euros into Norwegian kroner and there was only 20 minutes until the flight left for Tromsø. I packed everything into the trolley and headed for the departure gate only to see Cathy's back receding into the distance – too far to call her and the 'GATE CLOSING' sign flashing on and off! Surely having got this far we would not miss the plane to Tromsø. The whole reason we were travelling on the Thursday was because it was Easter and there were no planes on the Friday! We really did not want to spend 36 hours in Oslo together with the cost of a hotel, especially with no sponsorship.

Then I glimpsed Cathy on her way back, obviously totally unaware of the time. I waved at her but she seemed oblivious to everything around her. Eventually she was close enough for me to attract her attention. We grabbed our belongings, went through security and quickly headed for Gate 21. We must have looked a sight racing along laden with rucksacks, jackets, cameras, computers and the rest – we looked at each other and said 'Well I suppose we could have come through here earlier.'

Yes, we made it, but needless to say we were the last to board the plane. Of course, it was now impossible to find two seats together and all the overhead lockers were full. The stewardesses came to our aid and the plane departed five minutes late. As we flew north, the ground became gradually whiter and whiter and you could see that the snow was getting thicker. Soon we were high above the clouds. It would be interesting to see what the snow conditions were like once we landed in Tromsø. Hopefully, Per Thore would be there to meet us and I sat thinking how great it would be to see him again. It would also be my first chance to introduce him properly to Cathy. They had spoken briefly on the telephone but Per Thore had been away on a trail so the conversation had been brief and to the point.

We landed and were watching for our bags when through the crowd Per Thore appeared striding towards me, tanned and smiling. He said loudly 'Rona, how are you?' and welcomed me with a huge bear hug. It was great – and so good to be back. The year slipped away. I introduced him to Cathy and they politely shook hands. We gathered our belongings and went in search of his car. Whilst driving us to his home, Per Thore explained that Tromsø was an island and it seemed that most places were on the coastline this far north.

We drove along the edge of the fjord, suddenly turning into a drive, past the first house, round the corner, up the hill... then there it was, a large house surrounded by other buildings and just to the right of it, set back a little, were the kennels housing all Per Thore's huskies. As we arrived Per Thore's four-legged partners barked a welcome – or was it a warning? They were to provide the power for our transport for the next few weeks.

To the left was his garden hiding under a very thick layer of snow – well, it was melting, but it was thick by UK standards. The interior of the house was all made of wood with large open spaces and walls of windows looking out over the fjord with the mountains of the mainland beyond, at that moment covered in snow. Soon spring would take a hold, the colours would return and sailing boats would foray out onto the water but, for now, there was the promise of more snow and an adventure which we now knew for certain had never been done before.

What was Per Thore like? He was one of those quiet, strong men – a man of few words who, you instinctively knew, completely understood his environment and was totally comfortable with anything it could throw at him. Patient, watchful, he would deal with anything untoward that happened. He was always first to notice if one of the dogs was in distress or a sled seemed to be heading in the wrong direction without its owner and would be off instantly, sprinting after it. On one occasion on the Charity Challenge the previous year, he'd jumped straight onto a snowmobile to catch the dogs before they could make it home several days before they were due. I never saw him lose his temper or shout in anger and he rarely spoke unless it was to give a direction or to stop you doing something that might harm one of the dogs.

For now, there were introductions to be made and I was pleased that, at last, I was to meet the person Per Thore had spoken so highly of the year before and whom he had telephoned daily, his wife, Hege. She was lovely, so warm and friendly. We were then introduced to his son, little Jomar, a Viking name meaning fast and strong, who was an absolute delight. Their eight-year-old daughter, Christine, was unfortunately away visiting her grandparents. I hoped we would have a chance of meeting her on our return. We sat drinking coffee and chatting, and slowly it emerged that whilst we had been worrying about the challenges we were having in Andorra and England, high inside the Arctic Circle in Norway, Per Thore had been having his own.

He had seen a picture of a sled used by a Norwegian musher at the time of the gold rush in Alaska, which was tied together rather than bolted, and had decided he would copy it for our expedition. There was less likelihood of them breaking if they were tied. However, the brakes had not worked correctly and the sleds had broken. He had rebuilt them, though the waterproof covers he had ordered arrived only a day before we did. Sometimes it feels as though it is harder to organise an expedition than to actually go on one. I wondered whether I would still agree with that statement once we returned. It would no doubt depend on whether our return was in triumph or defeat.

Suddenly, Hege got up and disappeared off to the kennels to feed all the dogs, 39 Alaskan Huskies, six of them puppies, whilst Per Thore disappeared into the kitchen to cook the meal. When Hege returned, we sat round the table eating a delicious reindeer stew, rice and home-made bread. After a long and tiring day what could be better than good food, good company and very pleasant surroundings? Once we had finished our meal, Jomar, aged two and a half, cleared the table, always politely thanking whoever had handed him something.

What I didn't know until later was that Per Thore had finished guiding his ATD trips and then gone straight off to do the Finnmark Race (350k). (Per Thore loved racing dog-sleds when he was not guiding tours.) He had returned home just in time to pick us up at the airport. He and Hege had had no time together before we arrived there to take him off for another two weeks or so. Hege would dearly have loved to come with us but there were two small children who needed their mother. As the time drew nearer for us to leave, I thought she became more and more upset – and who could blame her? However, she never said a word. It must have been really tough for her.

Now the team was in one place we had to pull together to make this expedition work. It had a truly international flavour to it: one Norwegian dog-sled racer, one British round-the-world yachtswoman and one South African mountaineer. Three nationalities from three different cultures and three different disciplines – the question was just how would we get on along the route? The only team building we would do was in these last few days by getting the last minute bits and pieces and packing up the sleds. Also very much in our team of seven, but not actually sledding with us, was Hege – she worked tirelessly to get a lot of the equipment prepared and ready for the expedition. Her cousin, Ryno, was also a team member as he would be helping us get the dogs, equipment and food to the expedition's start point. Back home in the UK we had Alex, the publicist, and Anna, who worked for Alex and who just happened to be Norwegian.

By now we had been up for eighteen hours and tomorrow Per Thore had a big day lined up for us. We had to check the sleds, the equipment, the provisions and we were to meet the most important members of the team: the dogs. So for now, it was time to sleep. Per Thore showed us to our rooms in the basement and, after unpacking just the barest of necessities, I was very quickly under the duvet and sound asleep.

The next morning over breakfast, Per Thore explained to us that this far north they have darkness from about 6 December until around 22 February, often seeing the Northern Lights sometimes as early as 4 p.m. Meanwhile, Jomar had been busy making pancakes for a delicious breakfast for us and he cleared the table again with just a little help from some adults. Then it was time for us to get to work, so outside we went to check all of our equipment.

Per Thore's new sleds, copied from the old drawing, were so much bigger and stronger than the ones we had used in Sweden. Being tied together rather than bolted, they took longer to make; but he felt they would be able to withstand the punishment of both the heavy load they were to carry and, if the sleds went over, being lifted time and time again. I helped Per Thore put the plastic coating on the runners which would make the sleds slide over the snow more easily. Then he busied himself attaching the brakes and, on top of the runners where we would be standing, he put rubber strips so that our feet could not slip off too easily.

Photo 3 — Finishing the sleds (see page 115)

The sleds were so different from the lightweight ones we had used on the Charity Challenge. Those were made of beech wood, which is very pliable, and had appeared to be very rickety – but they had only had to carry a very light load. In fact, we found out that they were actually quite strong and that being rickety saved them from breaking. They looked rather like a low-slung child's buggy with a cover so that we could protect our rucksacks.

However, both types of sled had a wooden handle like a pram. At the right-hand corner was a wooden spike set on which, attached by a long piece of rope, was an ice anchor. This consisted of a metal handle from the ends of which curved two very large, sharp, menacing points which you pushed into the ground to hold the sled and your team of dogs from venturing further. At the back of the sled in between the runners were the brakes – yes, there were two of them. One was a band of metal (three sides of a rectangle) with two very sharp prongs at the corners which was attached to the lower part of the sled and held up against the back of it by a small length of bungee elastic. When you wanted to stop, you raised your foot and pushed this brake down into the snow. However, on the new expedition sleds there was a further brake, called a snowmobile brake. This was a rectangular piece of rubber with ridges on it which was also held up against the back of the sled. When you wanted to slow down you put your foot on it and pressed your weight down (well, I had to), which was a more gentle form of braking. Once you had managed to stop the sled the ice anchor was thrust into the snow to hold it firm. Co-ordination would be imperative.

Whilst Per Thore finished the sleds, Hege dealt with the dogs, and Jomar had his own mini adventures while Cathy and I tried to find our way around what would be our home for the next two weeks – a very nice tent. We only made one mistake whilst assembling it, getting the inner back to front which we very quickly rectified. Now was definitely the time to sort out all problems rather than when we were cold, tired and needing shelter. Just as we finished, it started to snow. Just what we wanted – and yes, I mean it, we really did want some more snow. As we arrived in Tromsø it had looked very much as it had done when we arrived in Kiruna, as though all the snow had gone – but we were wrong. There was plenty up in the mountains and more was promised. Per Thore and Hege have a very large, open garden and Jomar, with Hege by his side, wanted to show us something in a slightly wooded area about 20 yards from where we had been working. It was the footmark of a moose that had walked past; definitely a first for me!

We checked the waterproof covers, which Hege then adapted so that they could be fitted onto the sleds. Whilst I wrote more in my journal, Cathy scanned the photographs we had been taking and Per Thore poured over the maps trying to work out what our route might be. They then synchronised their GPS equipment to help us find our way and also to enable the website to be updated whilst we were on the expedition. Per Thore then explained how we would deal with getting fluid. We would have to boil snow to fill both the water bottles and a thermos. We were to drink a lot in the morning tailing off towards the end of the day. In the evening we would have to boil more snow to fill the thermos so we had a hot drink for the morning. That way we would pee during the day and might thus be able to get through the night without having to leave the tent during the coldest hours – so obviously sensible, when someone points it out to you. But, as Per Thore said, if we did want to go to the toilet at night we had to put our boots on and go a couple of metres from the tent. He explained that the reason for this was that the body uses up a lot of energy trying to keep its waste products warm; so you need to get rid of them as soon as possible in order to be able to sleep and thus perform well the next day.

Photo 4 – Per Thore and the maps (see page 116)

Having dealt with the waste production line, next there were the menus to sort out. The dogs would eat the same thing every day but variety for us would make the expedition more palatable. We needed to eat a lot of calories to ensure we had the energy to keep warm and sled the following day. We also had to ensure that the Primus was working. Sitting in the lounge looking out of the window, whilst making notes for this book, I could see cross-country skiers passing by. It was all so surreal and a far cry from the bustling world of Oxford. There was still a lot to do and we hadn't even been near a husky yet, and Cathy had never actually driven a dog-sled before. The plan was that if we could get everything else done then, hopefully, we would take the dogs out for a practice that afternoon; but with any expedition like this, it is always the organisation that takes the time. Well, didn't I know that!

As Per Thore said, once you are off on the trail, the shoulders go down and you can relax and just get on with it. Cathy and I were already beginning to relax – we had left the UK and our normal cares behind. For us, to a large extent the expedition started as we arrived in Tromsø. Well it certainly did for me: what I hadn't got with me, I would have to go without. In two days, the same would apply to Per Thore. By now we knew that the Primus worked, the waterproof covers were done and in place, so Per Thore and Cathy had a chance to mark the maps. Our starting point would be an hour-and-a-half's drive from Per Thore's house.

Checking the maps was certainly an education for me. I followed most of the route we were hoping to take but, with so many maps (it looked about 40 to me), so many imponderables (we were trying to open a dog-sled route to the northernmost tip of Norway) and so many contour lines, I got lost. I studied Geography and English Literature for my degree as a mature student but still I manage to get lost when driving from A to B. Although I trek a lot, I need to ponder over the map for quite a while before I can orientate myself. There are those who wonder how I ever managed to circumnavigate the world when I cannot find my way off the Manchester Inner Ring Road – but then on the yacht I had seventeen other people with me and I didn't do the navigating. Anyway, an extreme simplification of our global navigation was 'Leave Southampton, hang a right and catch the wind'. How we were going to find our way when the whole area was hidden deep beneath a very large amount of snow completely baffled me.

Some of the maps to Nordkapp were missing, so a shopping list was gradually evolving. Whilst we pondered over the maps, Hege was hard at work with her sewing machine making insulating bags to put round very large plastic containers. This would prevent all our food smelling of dog food. Insulation was put on the lid and held in position with duct tape. These insulated bags

Photo 5 – Hege worked tirelessly to get everything done

would be filled with the dog food, which is reindeer meat combined with fat. The food comes in large frozen blocks and probably the messiest job was when Per Thore took an electric saw to cut each one down into more manageable blocks. Slowly, one by one, everything was being accomplished.

It was a hive of activity but we still needed to update the website, and this I left to Cathy:

9 April – Final logistics in Norway

Our first day in Norway and the expedition is already beginning to feel like a reality. The morning has been spent on logistical chores – final touches to the sleds (which Per Thore made from scratch), including fitting brakes (a good idea given how energetic the dogs are), fitting the sled bags on the sleds, pitching the tents to check everything is in place, testing the Primus stoves, making insulating covers for the food boxes, and finding the 1:50 000 maps that cover our route (some 20 in all). This afternoon, if all goes well, we take the dogs for a spin. Then things really get exciting!!

I needed to make notes so that I had something to refer to when I started to write this book: I certainly wouldn't be able to remember everything. As each issue was dealt with, photographs had to be taken and reports written. I walked into the kitchen to take a photograph of Hege at the sewing machine, whilst Per Thore was cutting rope and splicing it for anchor ropes and release ropes, both very necessary with the number of dogs and heavy loads the sleds would be carrying. Meanwhile, back in the lounge, Cathy was testing our expedition computer by writing a report for the website. Then out came the satellite phone so that she could upload the report onto the website. It did not run smoothly: she had found a glitch. With a look of concentration on her face, Cathy gradually worked out the problem. At one point she turned towards the satellite phone with an expression that said 'Phone, do as I command.' However, the problem turned out to be that the www.explorersweb.com server at the other end was down, which was a real relief – at least it was not a problem at our end.

Lunch (yes, with all that work it was still only lunch time) was spaghetti bolognese made with reindeer meat, after which Per Thore gave us our Arctic suits and boots. Now the time had come to see just how well we could sled. I thought back to the previous year when this moment had arrived: kitted out in our Arctic attire we had gingerly stepped outside for our one and only lesson. In the interests of the animals' safety during our practice, the sled had been pulled by Digger (the Doctor we had to take with us for safety reasons) with Per Thore running by the side, holding on and telling us what to do. We had a small run along flat ground, turned 90° to the right to go up a small hill then turned another 90° at the top again to the right; then we went along this gradually downward sloping side, turned another 90° to the right and down the rest of the hill finishing with yet another 90° turn to be ready for the next person. Eventually it had been my turn to learn and practise how to sled, but by now it was Sid (the Leader for this trail – Per Thore was the Guide) pulling the sled with Per Thore running at the side. Now I'm not good on that white slippery stuff they call snow and ice, so I had been somewhat apprehensive as I started off but I quickly got used to it – or so I thought. However, that must have been the adrenaline because when I got off at the end my whole body just shook like a leaf.

On this expedition, Cathy and I would each have eight dogs whilst Per Thore would have ten in case one of them was injured. We collected the new sleds and took them through the dog pen and out to the other side. The ice anchors were put into the snow and release ropes tied to trees. We harnessed the dogs and then attached them to the ganglines on the sleds. The gangline is a line that runs between the dogs and is attached to the sled. Once the dogs are harnessed they are attached to the gangline by wires – one attached to the neck of the harness and one to the back of the harness near the tail. Soon we were ready to go. Perhaps because I was with Per Thore, whom I trust implicitly, I wasn't as scared as I had been in Sweden or in Andorra; but I was a little apprehensive because, where we were, there wasn't much snow. However, the sleds were empty which meant that the dogs would be able to go quite fast; and whilst we were harnessing the dogs, the snow started to fall.

Photo 6 – The rest of the team (see page 116)

By the time we were ready to go it had turned into a good snow shower. In fact, it became so heavy that we could hardly see where we were going. Per Thore took us quite a long way to test the sleds thoroughly, see how I was sledding this year and to give Cathy some real practice. I very nearly had a wipe out; but whereas last year I would have fallen, I managed to save myself. My sled took on a lot of snow and I not only managed to kick it away but, a little further on, I bent down to clear it away and also managed to pick up the release rope as it trailed next to the sled. This was definitely an improvement on my previous practice. Finally, I was beginning to feel at home again on the sled, the skills were coming back and I was becoming more confident and pleased with myself. I had also managed to guide the sled to the right and left – definitely new skills.

This was so different from our practice last year in Sweden. When all is going well and there is thick snow on the ground and in the skies, there is nothing more romantic than dog-sledding. I certainly had different feelings from last year. I was really beginning to enjoy myself and look forward to this expedition.

When I was first told about the Cancer Research UK dog-sled challenge, the thought had gone through my mind 'Wow, now that sounds exciting and romantic!' The comment posted on the website for our penultimate day was:

9 April – Running the dogs

Cathy: this afternoon we took the dogs out for a practice run, running empty sleds with six dogs each. It was one of the most romantic experiences of my life. We were running across crisp fresh snow, with groves of black trees standing stark under a grey-white sky. Flakes of snow were drifting past, as plump as spring blossoms. The dogs were padding silently, running hard and fast. Resisting all attempts to slow or brake. One of the joys of mushing is that the dogs are clearly enjoying it as much as the people. I can't wait to get started on the main event.

But no-one seemed to enjoy sledding more than little Jomar. As we arrived back at the house the snow ceased, we unharnessed the dogs and returned them to their rightful kennels whilst Hege harnessed her sled. Everyday Hege and Jomar went dog-sledding into the mountains beyond their garden, partly for fun but also to exercise the dogs and to train the puppies, with Jomar standing in the sled shouting 'Faster Mummy faster' (in Norwegian of course). Soon she was off with Jomar half-hidden in the sled crying out instructions (in Norwegian) as they sped along. In fact, Jomar had his own sled and was already capable of dog-sledding with one dog. A very different upbringing from that of my children, back in the UK.

Photo 7 – Hege and Jomar returning from a training run (see page 117)

'Hege is the most amazing woman.' Those were Per Thore's words and I can only agree. She had worked relentlessly to help get all the equipment and food ready in time, as well as keeping little Jomar amused and providing us with some amazing meals, all seemingly effortlessly. However, as I got to know Hege better she revealed that when Jomar was six months old she had been hospitalised with Guillain-Barre Syndrome which meant that she was completely paralysed and on a respirator for three months. Once the feeling started to return to her body she had had to learn how to do absolutely everything again and that included walking and talking. Now after two years she had still not completely recovered, there was still some loss of feeling particularly in her feet. She has to be one of the bravest women I know and Per Thore is incredibly supportive and always shows amazing love and concern for her. Now I understood why he had spent so much time on his mobile phone to her when we were on the trail for Cancer Research UK.

It had been a most productive day. At times we had worked on our own, at others we had worked together as a team to get the jobs finished. Discussing the menu we decided we would have porridge for breakfast, then we decided that as the dogs must come first we would deny ourselves the pleasure and maybe let the dogs have the porridge!

The day before we left to start the expedition, the three of us set off for the shopping malls of Tromsø. The sun was shining and the mountains across the water looked magnificent. We had a long shopping list to obtain the last-minute food, nuts and bolts, string, maps, and other oddments. I felt very sure that this year, with Per Thore in charge, we would not return home without everything we needed for the trail. The previous year whilst preparing for the Charity Challenge, I had dashed into town late in the afternoon (before leaving at four the next morning) to do my last-minute shopping, part of which was to buy a new head torch. I always have lots of different batteries at home so had decided I wouldn't waste money buying any more: I was sure to have the relevant one at home. Did I check the type of battery I would need whilst I was in the shop? No. When I arrived home and finally got around to checking the battery, it was clear that I didn't have the right one and by then the shops were shut. Never mind, I thought, I'll be able to buy one at the airport. I arrived at Heathrow to meet my fellow Charity Challenge dog-sledders and once in the departure lounge I went off in search of the battery. Needless to say, they had every kind except the one I wanted. Was there a crisis arising? It was apparently a unique battery and rechargeable. I was so annoyed with myself – I had been determined that this time I would have everything ready and not need to do anything at the last minute. But luck was not my friend. Two of my fellow dog-sledders (both from bonnie Scotland) were a hoot and ribbed me about it non-stop.

Since returning from our mini training session, it had been snowing constantly – the weather in the Arctic changes quite dramatically. We had packed most of the food, the insulating bags had been finished and the dog food (the frozen reindeer meat) had been chain-sawed into submission. We tested packing the sleds after yet another delicious meal which was probably going to be the last one for us for a while.

I decided that the illness I'd had earlier on in the week whilst still in the UK was a panic attack and I must have been having another one then as I became very well acquainted with the bathroom! I had been afraid that I would not be able to do this expedition, afraid that I would not be able to keep up. I was very much aware that both Cathy and Per Thore were much younger and I didn't want to hold them up, I was so determined to play my part. Cathy on the other hand had never had any doubt that she would be able to do this. In fact, on the Friday when we took the dogs out for a practice her sled tipped and she told me she nearly fell off three times but managed to rectify the sled each time whereas, if that had been my first outing on a dog-sled, I am pretty sure that I would have fallen over. She is a very keen skier so I suppose that does give her a bit of an advantage.

With virtually everything ready for the start of the expedition, we had an early night. All the preparations were certainly catching up with me. In fact, Cathy and I had had a snooze on the couches in the living room after dinner. I headed for bed and repacked my big bag with everything I did not need for the expedition and tried to get everything else into my very tightly packed rucksack. Even paring everything down to the bare essentials, I still felt I should have brought a slightly larger rucksack. My bed was welcoming and I soon slipped between the sheets and was very quickly safely asleep.

Before Cathy went to bed she updated the website once again:

10 April — 12 Hours and Counting...

After a morning spent shopping for food and other last-minute items, and an afternoon spent packing bags and boxes, we are ready to move out first thing tomorrow. The messiest job was packing the dog meat into containers. It comes in great frozen slabs of reindeer meat and fat that have to be cut down into manageable chunks with a chainsaw. Although it snowed for most of the afternoon where we are on the coast, reports from inland promise excellent conditions. We may face some snow and wind in the next few days, but on a long trip we can expect to meet every kind of weather. It is time for bed, one last night with the comfort of mattress, pillow and duvet, and 10 hours to enjoy every moment of it.

CHAPTER 4

Zero Hour

As morning dawned everyone got up – three of us were to have our last shower for some time. I repacked my rucksack yet again as, typically, overnight I had realised where I could economise and what else I would need. However, it was still a very tight fit. I hoped I wouldn't need to retrieve anything it contained in too much of a hurry. Little did I know how futile that hope would prove to be! The last-minute maps, with the dog names on the reverse for each sled, were completed; the strings were put into the final insulating bags. Then it was time to pack everything into Per Thore's truck.

Finally, we were ready. We sat drinking coffee until Hege's cousin, Ryno, arrived – he was going to help us with the dogs and at the start. The idea was to drive to Signaldalen, pack the sleds, walk the first part of the trail to see what the conditions were like then harness the dogs and set off. Hege and Jomar would come a little way with us and Ryno would film the beginning whilst other friends would help get the sleds up the first mountain. Ryno would then take that initial film back down the mountain and get it couriered to England for us. It was on this first part of the trail that 'the experienced mushers of Norway' thought the sleds would break as we had to weave our way up the mountain through the forest in thick snow. They thought the sleds were too heavy and that Cathy and I were too inexperienced. Would they be proved right? Now it wouldn't be long before we knew.

Our little convoy set off. It was going to take us a couple of hours to drive to Signaldalen past vast fjords and high mountains. Once there, the road into the valley seemed to go on and on but, finally, we arrived at our starting point. Removing the sleds from the trailer, we loaded them up. We had met with Tom Frode en route who had confirmed that the Three Nations Border was 'looking good'. This was, we hoped, to be our first campsite of the expedition. The plan was for Ryno to film the start and then ride on a snowmobile past us, filming us as we gradually wound our way through the forest. We took photographs of all the action as the sleds were loaded and the dogs harnessed as well as some video clips and eventually dogs, sleds and team were ready. The safety lines were tied to the bumpers of the truck and cars as, once harnessed, the exuberance of the dogs to set off just couldn't be denied. They yapped and barked and tugged frantically at those harnesses. Some of them were jumping up and down on the spot, trying desperately to get going. They just loved to run.

This reminded me so much of the start of the Charity Challenge. As soon as lunch was over we had packed our kit into the sleds and the guys running the Musher's Lodge had helped us to harness all the dogs. Once that was accomplished - we had been told to stand at the front and hold the two lead dogs until everyone was ready. Then we had to get onto the runners at the back with one foot firmly on the brake, pick up the ice anchor and wait. Because the dogs loved to run and knew they were about to set off, the noise of their barking had been deafening. Each of the 'volunteers' had four dogs in their team, whilst Sid and Digger each had six, their sleds had held the supplies of our food and equipment, as had Per Thore's but he had had ten dogs. This had been in case a dog was injured and had to be replaced – the injured dog would then have ridden on top of one of the sleds. That meant that we had had 70 dogs harnessed and desperate to run; not only that but all the other dogs in the kennels had wanted to come with us, so they had been bouncing up and down and creating a din. You just weren't able to hear yourself think.

It was time to say our farewells and we walked away to check our sleds for the last time so that Per Thore and Hege could say a private farewell.

Jomar waved and Hege smiled the smile of someone who is being left behind whilst others head off on an adventure. Much later, when Per Thore and I were chatting as we sled along, he told me the hardest part of any trail for him was saying goodbye to Hege and leaving her behind. As we were about to set off, I was full of excitement but I couldn't help wondering whether we would really be able to accomplish our goal. Per Thore decided it was time we should leave. The 26 dogs made a tremendous racket. This was the first time I had driven eight dogs. With Cathy and I standing on the runners of our sleds, firmly clinging on to the safety ropes attached to the sleds and looped around the bumpers of the trucks and passed back to us, and with the ice-anchors lodged carefully on the uprights, we were now ready to slip the ropes and go. We waited for our cue...

The start of any expedition is thrilling. Electricity courses through your veins as you wait in anticipation. Suddenly, without a word, we were off. It happened so fast – all the worries and anxieties and the challenges flew

Photo 8 – Let's get going!

Photo 9 – The final preparations

out of my head. Now was the time to concentrate on the here and now. Per Thore led the way, I followed with Cathy bringing up the rear. The trail turned and twisted as we ran along the valley and then started to ascend through the wood. The excited rush soon dissolves into thin air as the reality of negotiating these heavy sleds up a steep narrow track that winds through the forest to a place 600 metres above the start reminds you that dog-sledding is far more difficult than it looks. We had to jump off the runners not only to make the load lighter for the dogs but to help them by running behind and pushing the heavy sleds, each weighing 120 kilos, up the track.

Having videoed the rush of the sleds at the start, Ryno went in front, racing up the mountain on a snowmobile, stopping at various vantage points to video us as we drove the dog teams higher and higher up the mountain. I am sure I looked a positive sight with my little Arctic hat and bright red sunglasses, but I didn't care, I was concentrating on my sledding. Although this certainly was not an easy route, I found that I had more control of the sled now and a lot more confidence. We hadn't been sledding for more than five minutes when Per Thore turned his head and called back 'Don't slow down, full speed and no braking!' Why had he shouted this instruction? Then I saw it! A little further ahead up the trail I could see we were heading towards a sharp right-hand bend and, at the apex of the bend, the trail sloped ominously to the right to a sheer drop of about 60 metres down the cliff-side. However, Per Thore was already past it. With my heart in my mouth I conveyed the same message back to Cathy then turned back to concentrate on what lay ahead. This was to be the first white-knuckle ride of the trail – get it wrong and the dogs, sled and Rona would be plunging down the cliff face with little chance of survival. I clenched my teeth, I was so scared – I had never attempted anything like this before. I shouted encouragement at my dogs – 'Go! Go! Go!'

I made it. It was exhilarating but I didn't dare think of what might have happened if I had chickened out and braked. Luckily, we all made it. I slalomed along the route avoiding trees and steep slopes. In fact, I even lay out to the left as the sled nearly went over to the right and managed to keep it upright. But then the inevitable happened. We jinked to the left and then the right, only I went a little too far and the sled and I hit the snow. I managed to get up but there was no way I could get the sled upright. I had the 'human food' in my sled and I felt as though I was letting the others down if I could not pick it up myself. As a friend remarked on my return, 'Rona, if you could pick up a sled twice your weight you would be in the Olympics!' Well I wish I had known that when I was on the expedition. However, Per Thore came back to help me and we were soon off again. Cathy was sledding like a pro – no doubt this was down to her skiing ability. I haven't skied since I was fifteen, some years ago now and I doubt whether I ever will again. Although every so often, she seemed to be a lot farther behind than I would have thought, only for me to realise that she had tipped her sled over as well. We went onward and upward until at last we stopped to say thank you and goodbye to Ryno as he handed over the video camera and took the first footage of our expedition back down the mountain. Here Hege and Jomar were waiting and the footage started its journey back to the TV companies in the UK.

We were really on our own now – it was all up to us. It was not until we returned to Tromsø that Ryno was to tell us that there had been eleven snowmobiles driving past us on their way down through the forest. I couldn't believe it. I certainly hadn't noticed them at all, so completely immersed was I in concentrating on keeping my sled in one piece. I was very aware of the expectations of those 'experienced mushers of Norway'. Would we fail? Would the sleds break as we wound our way through the forest? We had proved them wrong on that point – but would we be able to prove them wrong about the rest of the trail?

The start had brought back memories of the Charity Challenge. Back then, we had been standing on the runners of our little sleds with only four dogs each when, again without a word, Per Thore had set off racing down the track and one by one we had followed. It had certainly been a baptism by fire. We had gathered speed as we sled down the steeply sloping track when without prior warning there loomed in front of us the tall forbidding frame of silent Taisto, standing ominously next to his snowmobile blocking our route. His eyes had watched how each one of us was treating his four-legged partners. Then we had realised that it was to ensure that we followed Per Thore – the only way for us to go had been to delve into the forest! We had gone over bumps, round 90° turns at what seemed like the most incredible speeds. Per Thore had disappeared round numerous bends happy to be off on the trail at last. Having had to wait for so long, the dogs had raced along. We had gone over moguls, round trees (mostly), up hills and down dales. Every so often one of us had overbalanced and the sled had tipped over with the sledder being deposited in a heap in the snow.

This meant the sledder had had to pick him- or herself up, try to retrieve the sled, get back on and set off once more. We had been told it was important that we stayed in line so if the person in front of you fell, you had to stop and wait until they were up and off once again. Stopping the dogs so someone could be reunited with their own sled had made the dogs bark louder and louder and the noise only subsided once they were allowed to run again. At first I had been really tense and scared of falling and so gripped the handle of the sled tightly; but the further we had gone the easier it became to adjust and work with the dogs and I had started to relax a little, or so I thought. We had had to stop constantly so that the others could catch up. Suddenly we had come out of the forest and gone down a long steep bumpy hill onto a frozen lake. It had been huge and, after the confines of the forest, it felt great to have a large flat expanse to sled on.

But back to the present: now it felt as though the expedition had really started – it was just the three of us plus dogs and we seemed to be doing quite well. Unfortunately, a little complacency on my part put an end to that: I wrapped my team around a tree which, inexplicably, had planted itself in the middle of our path – another case of Per Thore having to come to my rescue. Suddenly we emerged onto the plateau, above the tree line, and were surrounded by rounded mountain tops. The silence was awesome – not a word I would normally use but the only one for the effect of that complete lack of sound. There we were, three different nationalities from three different disciplines with three different cultures and just snow, sleds and silence.

We soon arrived at a very pretty area with lots of large rocks showing through the snow. Allowing the dogs to run at their own pace, they simply flew whenever there was a downhill. I had to brake frantically as the gangline kept going slack. We crested a hill and, when Per Thore turned to check his team, he could see Cathy trying to coax her dogs along. Her sled had come to a halt in thick snow. We stopped and waited; then Per Thore said he would look after my dogs and I was to go back to help her. This was where I realised the efficiency of a sled – once you get off the sled runners, you sink up to your thighs in snow. This was definitely not the easiest way of walking down a steep hill. I found Cathy pulling, pushing and tugging at her sled, anything to get it going. I tried to pull the sled – nothing. We both had a go but for all our pulling, pushing and tugging, our combined strength still would not shift it. I tried to lift it to the side but still no luck. I went to the back of the sled again. There had to be a way to make it move.

I looked down, checking everything to see if I could see the problem. Hey presto! There it was – she had put her foot on the brake and it was now stuck in the deep snow. Well, at least we knew that the brake worked properly. I kicked it a few times to release the compacted snow surrounding it and then tugged the sled slightly sideways and she was off up the hill as fast as the dogs could go. However, I was still back where she had come to a standstill. It was an even harder trudge up the hill back to my sled, pulling each leg out of the deep snow at every step. I was exhausted, but I grabbed a drink and we were off again. Uphill, down dale, waving at the odd snowmobile-rider along the way until we eventually arrived at our first frozen lake by the Three Nations Border where Norway, Sweden and Finland meet.

Whilst we had our lunch, we sat in each country in turn then helped a stranded snowmobile rider to get going again before we got back onto our sleds to find a place to camp for the night. We tried to go into the forest but the snow was far, far too deep so we had to turn round and eventually Per Thore decided the only place to camp was by the edge of the forest on the side of the lake. He put the chains out and we unharnessed the dogs. Each time we took a dog from the sled to the chains we were sinking thigh deep in snow – it took a long time to unharness all of them. This was certainly not the easiest of places to camp. Per Thore then drilled two boreholes in the frozen lake for water, one for the dogs and another one for us so that the two were

Photo 10 — Preparing the dogs' supper

kept separate. Each day we had to ladle 75 litres of water from the borehole for the dogs, and ten litres for us. This chore fell to me on that first day. I would fill up one of the insulated bags and carry it all the way back to the campsite. Sometimes the borehole would be over a hundred metres away and there would be thick snow to cross before I could put the water into a metal container to which Per Thore would add the frozen reindeer meat that he had chopped up with the axe. He would then set fire to a cloth underneath it and boil the water and meat to make a very thick soup for the dogs to which he would add some dried dog food.

Each day the 26 dogs would eat 20 kilos of reindeer meat mixed together with 75 litres of water to which was added 20 kilos of dried food to make the soup. So each evening we would make enough for their supper and for their breakfast the next morning, putting half into the insulated containers where it was kept overnight. (See Appendix 4 – Dog-sledding Facts.) Only once the dogs had been fed could we think about ourselves and about putting up the tents and preparing our own meal. The dogs always came first, no matter what. But now they were fed it was time for us.

We were in an extremely exposed spot and so decided that, once the tents were up, we would try to shelter them as much as possible with the sleds. With the tents erected we could then dig a hole inside, shovelling snow onto the outside skirt of the tent to help hold it down before off-loading our food into the front part of the tent and preparing our own meal. After chatting for a short while, we went to bed but not before Cathy had given me a lesson on how to go to the toilet when there is no cover and you want to retain just a little dignity. However, my timing was not good and I ended up with a very cold bottom. We slid into our welcoming sleeping bags and whilst I wrote my journal, Cathy tried to update the website but there seemed to be yet another glitch. Eventually she managed to send a dispatch – our first one from the trail.

Finally, we both snuggled down to sleep as the wind increased, howling round the tents on their exposed snowy plateau. It had been a great day – fantastic sledding, the real thing and a very far cry from last year's trail – but now we were exhausted and this was only the first day. The pressure of the preparations and the anticipation had taken their toll and we knew we would have to be up for a fairly early start tomorrow.

Our timing seemed to be out that Monday morning. For some reason, I expected Per Thore to be up bright and early, but he had said that he hated getting up in the morning and that night he had been disturbed by two Finnish women who were skiing and could not find their cabin. Eventually we had breakfast, prepared sandwiches for lunch, packed up the tents and sleds and harnessed the dogs. It was very windy where we had camped but now all was ready and we could retrace our steps to get back on the trail. We had taken a detour so that we could visit the Three Nations Border – thinking it would be a memorable place – but it turned out to be just a very large stone, which was somewhat disappointing to say the least, although I suppose it did mark a memorable spot. Once back on the trail, slowly and surely, we started to climb a mountain. We had been camping at 500 metres and now had to go up to 800 metres. It was a very hard slog.

The ground undulated as we sled up the mountain. We had to jump off the sleds and run up the slope pushing them to help the dogs; then as the ground fell away, we'd jump back on so that we could brake to stop the sleds running onto the back of the dogs. Anyone who thought we would just stand on the runners and let the dogs do the work would have been in for a very big shock indeed. Not only would the dogs have been so exhausted that they would not have been able to finish the trail but it would have incurred the wrath of Per Thore – no-one was allowed to do anything to harm the dogs. After all, they were our engines and of paramount importance. Sledding also requires total concentration: as soon as you stop, for example, the dogs will go off to the left or right and you will be off the sled or, worse still, it will have tipped over and you will be dragged along the trail – as had happened last year.

Then, we had been caught in a whiteout at Soppero where the wind-chill plummeted to -30°C. It had been too dangerous for us to sled and, when we had started again, the trail had been like a sheet of ice. We had raced along the trail until it took a sharp left-hand bend around a tree, so if I had leant to the left as I should have done I would have hit my head on the tree. Trying

Photo 11 – Time to get up Photo: C. O'Dowd

to avoid a collision, I had stayed a little too upright and the roots had tipped my sled, dislodging me from the runners. Our instructions at the beginning had been that if we fell off the sled we should not let go as the dogs would be off over the horizon. With the sled now on its side and me hanging on (as instructed – would I dare to let go?) the dogs gradually realised that something was amiss. As soon as they had come to a standstill, I had started to get to my feet, lifting the sled at the same time. However, this had reduced the resistance on the sled so the dogs had immediately set off again. Very quickly I had pulled the sled back down again – I had not had time to get to my feet at all. I was then dragged along the trail again doing a wonderful impression of superman on my stomach. All the time this had been happening, the ice anchor had been bouncing along with its two very large sharp prongs only centimetres from my face. Try as I might, I could not co-ordinate lifting the sled once the dogs had stopped, getting into an upright position and back onto the runners before the dogs had started again. When the dogs had finally stopped I just laid there giggling. The thought went through my head that I might have to finish the day in the prone position. Paul had been on the sled behind me watching the whole scenario and when he had finally stopped laughing he had asked me whether I needed any help. My knight in shining armour anchored his sled, picked mine up, putting the ice anchor into the trail whilst I got back on my feet and rejoined the sled. Once Paul was convinced that sled and body were reunited he asked whether I was ready, held the sled and, whilst I had both feet on the brake, gave me the ice anchor and let go – and I caught up with the front of our group.

So as you can see, timing is of the utmost importance and with the sleds the previous year being very light I was really pleased to have had Paul there to help. However, the weight of our sleds now, forced on us of necessity as Per Thore had really wanted a six-person team, was part of the challenge. This trail was certainly going to be no easy matter. If I had managed to get more people, the sleds could have been lighter but – dare I say? – I was really enjoying the fact there were only three of us.

As we travelled across the mountain range the scenery was breathtaking – blue skies above with the sun shining and glinting on the crisp snow as we passed. There was a sheet of white as far as the eye could see and just three sleds, 26 dogs, Per Thore, Cathy and me. Apart from the whoosh of the runners, the pitter patter of the dogs' feet and the ha-ha-ha of their breathing there was no noise at all. Just complete silence.

Eventually we made it to the top of the mountain and now the only way was down. Climbing up is tough, really hard work. Even Per Thore with all his experience thinks so and he is a Norwegian ex-Special Forces Paratrooper and an extremely fit man. Traversing the top is blissful, but going down is a complete nightmare. The dogs are wanting to race straight down, it is usually bumpy and they are totally unaware now that the heavy sled is catapulting after them. More to the point, so am I. As the sled is so heavy, it tries to go faster than the dogs; consequently the gangline goes slack and can cause severe injury to the dogs, as had happened on the Charity Challenge, so you have to brake just enough to ensure that the gangline stays taught but not too much so that you hold up the dogs. The dogs cannot understand why you are braking and look back at you as if to say 'What's the matter, why won't you allow us to go faster?' As you fly down the mountainside you have not only to concentrate on the gangline and the brake but you have to think about the route. If the route moves to the left you have to lean to the left, the sled being desperate to fall to the right and vice versa. Consequently you are throwing your weight from one side to the other. If it's very steep then you need both feet on the brake and you're being bounced over moguls – mind that rock on the left! You need to lean to the right to move the sled away from it.

So what had happened last year with the gangline? Well, as we had neared the end of a day's sledding we had raced down a hill onto yet another frozen river. Whilst they had made great 'roads' for us, this one had been in the open countryside and was totally unprotected as a storm started to brew; so, as our sleds were very light, we had been immediately blown to the edge of the river where the snow was deep and soft. The wind was incredibly strong and the wind-chill had dropped to -20°C. It had been unbelievably difficult to sled but there was nothing that we could do to stop the sleds slipping on the icy snow. Even the dogs had been blown backwards – we had been out of control.

Then, disaster! Moira had been sledding in front of me and her dogs were running slightly slower than mine so, as we sled along the track, I was continually braking as my dogs had tried to overtake Moira's sled, or had had their noses either hard on her heels or through her legs. As we had turned to go up the river bank to our lodge for that night, Moira's dogs had dashed to the left and then suddenly slowed drastically. Mine had been so close that they were on top of Moira's sled, which was then stuck in relatively deep, soft snow before she could get going again. My dogs had been following the line hers had taken for the whole of the trail and now was no exception. They turned back on themselves and that's when the accident happened. My dog, Pria, got her leg caught in the gangline at exactly the same time as my lead dogs, Domni and Samni, had taken off; immediately the gangline had tightened round the middle of Pria's leg. I had stamped on the brake hoping that the slight stop would be enough to slacken the gangline and release her leg. It had very nearly succeeded as the gangline had opened slightly and slipped down Pria's leg. However, she had just not been quite quick enough before the dogs had taken off again and the gangline had tightened round the end of her paw. Although I had tried to put the ice anchor in it hadn't held in the soft snow.

I had quickly turned and called to Carol, who was sledding behind me, to move up and hold my sled so that I could run forward and release Pria's paw but in the confusion she had thought I wanted her to hold the ice anchor and, deciding she wasn't strong enough she had moved forward to hold the dogs! Brave woman. However, by then Pria had been in so much pain that she had bitten Pippa, the dog harnessed next to her, in a mistaken effort to make her stop pulling the sled. There had been no way that Pria could get Domni and Samni to stop and they were determined to continue up the bank following Moira's sled.

Pria and Pippa had been biting each other hard and there had been blood everywhere. I had started to panic – I shouted for more help and Paul, who had been a couple of sleds behind me but still on hard snow, anchored his sled and ran forward. It had been impossible for me to hold my sled and release Pria's paw. Paul had managed to do it but by now his dogs had managed to get loose and were on their way up the bank. Catching his sled just in time, he had jumped on and continued up the bank. Once we had arrived at the top of the bank we had unharnessed the dogs. As soon as everyone was safely off the frozen river, the sleds had been carefully stowed and the dogs fed, Per Thore and I had had an opportunity to check my injured dogs. Both had got deep cuts which had gone through muscles which caused a lot of concern. However,

Pria had had a tear on one leg which required stitches. To my astonishment Per Thore had put these in by means of a stapler – it had made me very pleased that we also had a doctor along for the humans!

Whenever the art of dog-sledding comes up, I always have the distinct feeling that some people think it is easy to do – that you just stand on the runners at the back of the sled and let the dogs pull you along. If only they knew the work you had to put in to this 'effortless' skill.

Well, back to the present, having gone up the mountain we did the scary part of coming down again on the other side. Cathy had been living in Andorra and skiing for the last three years, so had plenty of opportunity to practise frequently. In fact, Per Thore rechristened her 'the downhill' as she went flying down the mountain only later confessing that she had fallen three times – at one time hitting her head on a rock. This was getting dangerous and I started to wonder whether my insurance was up-to-date. Eventually we had a five-minute stop part of the way down the mountain where it was somewhat flatter; just time enough to eat some lunch before continuing down to the bottom. However, this was not before Cathy's dogs had decided to visit mine. I caught them and we put the ice anchor back in, only a little more firmly this time. For once, I managed to stay upright as we flew down the mountain but, looking across the valley that we were about to traverse, my apprehension was, to say the least, heightened. I was beginning to wonder why I had ever agreed to this expedition. As we set off again, Per Thore made sure to tell us to take it easy and go one at a time. This was not a race.

Having navigated our way to the bottom of the mountain, we crossed a lake and then we came to the tricky part: in front of us was a road which had to be crossed. There are very few roads this far north in Norway but, like geographical arteries, they are essential to the people who live here. We were to come across one or two before we found ourselves completely away from civilisation in the mountains of the far north. Per Thore told me to anchor my sled and walk over the road, to tell him when it was clear for him to take his sled across. Luckily, we were at a spot where there was quite a long clear stretch of straight tarmac but, needless to say, what traffic there was, was going fast. I would certainly need my knowledge of the dogs to get the timing right: a sled plus ten dogs becomes a very long vehicle, easily the length of a coach, and difficult to manoeuvre as the dogs don't always want to go in a straight line. I felt rather honoured that Per Thore should rely on me – but then, it was certainly better that he undertake this tricky manoeuvre of driving the sleds across the road rather than us.

Photo 12 – Navigating the tarmac highway (see page 117)

Once all was clear I indicated for him to come. It was a difficult crossing. From where Per Thore was, the sleds were in a large dip in a deep and bumpy part of the trail and they were heavy so the dogs would take a moment or two to get moving. The weight of the sled stopped them momentarily before they came up the rise onto the road. This would have to be crossed at an angle before navigating round a very large mound of snow on the other side, round a corner and down an incline before he could harness his team securely and return to repeat the manoeuvre with the next sled. I kept look out as he came across and disappeared into the valley.

Eventually he reappeared, plodding up the trail having anchored his sled and tied it to a tree. Next he got on my sled and brought it closer to the road and waited. As soon as it was clear I called to him to come but suddenly, round the corner came a fast-moving lorry. I shouted to him to stop. The lorry passed and I waited. When it was clear again he drove my team across the road, but they decided to go over the hard lump of snow rather than round it making me wonder whether some of my problems could be due to them and not me! It was quite reassuring to see Per Thore having a challenge with them. With the precision of an engineer he kept the sled upright but the dogs got confused and stopped, straddled across the road.

We had to get them clear before another vehicle came hurtling round the corner. I ran up to them and pulled the first two round and onto the trail and Per Thore disappeared into the valley again. Several cars and lorries had passed and they were certainly moving fast. Now we only needed to get Cathy's sled across. Once again Per Thore brought it closer to the road and waited. I couldn't get over the fact that he had such trust in me to help him with this tricky crossing. Again we waited until the road was clear; Cathy could get across before the dogs. I indicated for him to cross but, as the first two dogs hit the road, another lorry came round the corner. I ran into the middle of the road and held my hands up hoping the lorry would stop, which luckily he did. I dread to think of the carnage if he hadn't. Once we were all reunited with our sleds, we set off to find our way up the next mountain. The trail was getting harder and required a considerable amount of mushing.

Just to clarify mushing for you, this is where you have one foot on the runner and you 'scoot' with the other foot. That is, you put your foot down on the snow and push hard to move the sled forward – it's a bit like skateboarding only with dogs at the front! So for guidance purposes, you have to mush whilst you are travelling on flat ground; jump off and run up mountains pushing a 120-kilo sled in front of you; and know the right moment to jump onto the runners and begin braking as you start to descend the mountain so that the sled does not run into the backs of the dogs and harm them. At the same time, as you go round corners you have to lean to the right or left, as appropriate (right-hand corners, lean to the right; left-hand corners, lean to the left), in order to stop the sled tipping over. And, yes, there is more. If you see an obstacle to your left you have to lean to the right to try to guide (yes, I did say try) the sled round the right hand side of it; and if you see an obstacle to the right you lean to the left. All this has to be done on the move, bringing a new meaning to 'thinking on your feet'. So you thought this was going to be an easy ride did you? Think again. You need the fitness of an extreme athlete to get it right which probably accounts for the spills (not the thrills) that I had.

At times, the hills were so steep that you would have to get off and walk whilst pushing the sled up to the top – although once you're off, the sled is lighter and so the dogs go faster. The trick is to judge the precise moment when you need to jump back onto the runners before the dogs are going so fast that you can't.

We were off the beaten track now and the scenery was incredible. The clouds made wonderful blue–grey shadows on the snow as they moved across the landscape. After a considerable amount of hard work, we came to a wide expanse of white – a frozen lake – at the far end of which was a cabin. This was to be our home for the night. We sled silently across the lake and stopped. We were close to the border with Finland at Loassomuvra. Cathy was some long way behind as one of her dogs was playing up and she was using the opportunity to take photographs. We put the chains out, and Cathy and I unharnessed our dogs and put them onto the chains. Cathy then unloaded my sled of all that we needed and took it into the cabin.

Photo 13 – The life-saving drill (see page 118)

Finding water here proved to be a bit of a challenge. Per Thore had brought a two-metre drill with him for boring through the snow and ice to get to water. So we always had to find a frozen river or lake to camp beside. According to the maps there should have been a river nearby, so Per Thore went one way and sent me off in another to look for it; but to no avail. The only possibility was the lake we had just traversed. Eventually, he bored a hole and found the golden nectar in the middle of the lake. The hole was only 15–20cm wide and it would take a long time to ladle those 85 litres of water into the containers and return to the campsite. I know because I ended up having to ladle that amount of water every evening (apart from this one) as soon as the dogs were unharnessed. On this particular day the borehole was a long way away and an insulated bag full of water is very heavy – I would have to fill a bag and carry it back to the campsite several times. But this day Per Thore decided that Cathy and I needed food before the dogs and started to cook for us. Cathy was very quiet and I wondered whether it was because she had hit her head coming down the mountain. She seemed very withdrawn. I went to help make the supper and Per Thore asked how I was. When I said that my back was hurting and the area between my thumb and first finger was hurting again, as it had done a year previously, Per Thore told me to relax more. He thought I was probably holding onto the sled too hard. Then Cathy said that her back was hurting and she had bruises on her hands. It had been a hard day for all of us and the dogs still needed to be fed.

After our meal we all went outside to get the job done. Cathy collected a bucket of water and stopped: she was definitely not her usual self. There were two more buckets of water needed for the evening meal and she went, I thought a little reluctantly, to go and collect them. Then she said that she had received an email saying that our technical equipment should now work, so Per Thore suggested that she go in and deal with it whilst I helped him with the dogs. Maybe it had been the technical equipment playing up again that had been the problem. By the time we had finished, Cathy was sitting in bed; and after going outside for the nightly toilet run she settled down for the night. There appeared to be something wrong, as she had not even attempted to help with the washing up or chat to Per Thore. However, earlier she had started to read out the various heights we had scaled that day, so I grabbed my notebook to take them down. After the washing up, I started to write my journal and Per Thore took himself to bed. Ah well, we would see what tomorrow held in store. Forty minutes after the dogs had been fed they all howled – it's their way of saying thank you for the food. But for now, with Per Thore and Cathy sound asleep, it was time for me to hit the sack. It was 9.50 p.m. and it had been a long day. We'd sled nearly twice as far as we had done on day one. Our dispatch from Cathy on the website read:

12 April – The going gets tough

We are tucked up warmly inside a cabin next to the Finnish border, at Loassomuvra. From 500 metres we pushed up over 800 metres, dropped down to cross the great lake of Gálggojávri at 500 metres and climbed back up to 800 metres. The ascents are hard work, mushing or running by the sleds. And the descents demand constant concentration and braking to stop the sleds running over the dogs.

Always the challenge is the weight of the sleds. As Per Thore says, they are shit-heavy (this being a technical mushing term, of course). Worst are traverse descents with the sleds tipping over precariously to one side. I went over three times in just 50 metres. The third time a cliff above was echoing the barking of my team and they were jumping about frantically in search of the ghost dogs, starting to run each time I levered the sled a few inches above the ground. At which point I would drop the sled and do a superman-style dive for the sled bar and the snow anchor. Hopefully, better luck tomorrow.

Except that tomorrow we lose the convenience of snowmobile trails and spend two days trail-breaking through soft snow. The challenge continues...

Well, at least Cathy was having the same problems as I was – although I didn't know that until after the expedition, back in the UK, as I didn't see any of the dispatches whilst we were away. Maybe it would have helped if I had. I had to get up in the middle of the night and the sky and land were as one, a creamy blue with a few gentle clouds and a few brilliant stars. Not long after I had snuggled back into my sleeping bag, the dogs started barking ferociously and howling. (Last year this would have meant the start of the sledders, woken by the dogs, taking it in turns to go to the toilet. This year, we were far too tired and the three of us slept on.) The dogs created an unearthly din. This usually denotes that something is going through the campsite – but in this case, exactly what it was would only be revealed in the morning.

The next day the alarm went off but nobody stirred. Gradually, one by one we surfaced, had breakfast, and then came a monumental moment for me, my first public crap –please excuse the language, the vernacular comes from my sledding mates. I had hoped that I would not need to do one at all but I suppose it comes to us all at some point. I managed quite well, I thought, for a beginner and wondered afterwards why I had been so worried about it. We fed the dogs, packed the sleds and harnessed the dogs. Cathy wrote all the dispatches on the trail and posted them onto the website as many of our supporters had asked whether they would be able to track our progress. It kept them up-to-date and enabled them to understand the amount of work we had to do when we were not actually sledding. That day's posting read:

Doggie dinner time

The logistics of keeping the dogs on the paw: We have 26 dogs, which we feed twice a day. They are burning up around 5,000 calories a day. To replace that we go through nearly a 20 kg pack of dry food a day, and 20 kg meat. To make the food we mix hot water, chopped meat, and dry food in vacuum boxes. Two of our three sleds are filled with dog food.

Each dog gets a two-litre bowl of food and water in the evening, and in the morning a 1/2 bowl. For the dogs we need 45 litres of water each evening and 30 litres each morning, plus 10 litres for three people. We simply can't melt enough snow each day to produce 85 litres. We need a liquid water source. We use an ice drill to drill down through a metre of snow and ice to access the water in the many lakes in the region. The dogs also eat snow as they run for water.

Hygiene is very important as we can easily contaminate our food with dog food and get sick. Human food and dog food are always kept on different sleds.

The sun was shining and the snow glistening as we set off the next day. It was a beautiful morning. There was nothing but sparkling mountains, blue sky and drifts of virgin snow with the contrast of an occasional black rock.

Two of my dogs had been exchanged with two of Cathy's in the hope that hers would go faster. As we moved off up the mountain, we crossed the only sign of life in this white wilderness, the footprints of an Arctic fox, rare in this area. This was obviously what had upset the dogs during the night. On top of the plateau it was beautiful but we very nearly crossed momentarily into Finland as the snow was being blown like sand in a desert, making it extremely difficult to see. Apparently, Per Thore told us later, there were border patrols. If we had trespassed into Finland and been caught we would not have been allowed out of the country as they have very stringent regulations about dogs. Luckily, we had only skimmed very close to the border in error.

Photo 14 — Shara's breakfast Photo: C. O'Dowd

We soon came upon a Norwegian reindeer fence which we had to negotiate. Part of it was broken and lying flat on the ground so we drove towards that. Per Thore went first but his sled got caught. I was very close behind so he pulled my dogs to the side and pushed them through. I put in the ice anchor as Cathy appeared with her dogs. She stopped and put her ice anchor in to go back and help Per Thore get his dogs through, at which point her dogs took off. I raced after them and much to my surprise, not only caught them, but also managed to stop them, which was odd as I usually had difficulty even trying to stop my own sled. Could it have been because Per Thore and Cathy carried the dog food and, whereas all the sleds weighed 120 kilos at the start, the dogs were eating a large amount of food each day – 40 kilos or more. My sled carried the human food and, though we were eating a lot, we were certainly not eating anywhere near that amount per day.

Photo 15 – The offending fence (see page 118)

Once Cathy's sled was secured, I went back to mine to find that one of the fence wires was caught in my brake. Per Thore managed to release it and we were off again. We went down one slope so fast that, although I had the gangline taut, the dogs hit a patch of soft snow and came to a halt on top of each other. As they set off again I realised that one of them, Varg, had caught his leg in the gangline. Memories of last year came flooding back – oh please no, not that scenario again! I stopped the sled and ran to Varg but, in order to release him, I had to pull the front four dogs back to slacken the line. The dogs immediately started to run as the ice anchor would not hold in the soft snow. Cathy gave me a lift on her sled. As my dogs drew near to Per Thore, he held up his hand and shouted at them. I knew they didn't dare pass him! As Cathy and I approached he told me to hurry to get back onto my sled. I got the feeling I was in disgrace because of my lack of control of dogs and sled.

As we travelled through this unfamiliar landscape, Per Thore would pore over the map and his GPS. At this point, we were not on a very steep slope and the sun was shining so we were running behind the sleds with our jackets flapping open in order to stop ourselves overheating, sweating with the exertion of pushing them when we went up a mountain. Soon we were at the highest point in the area, on top of the Haalti Mountains. At this height, the wind was whipping the snow off the ground making it into a cloud swirling over the mountain top. The temperature plummeted and this bitter, bitter wind blew the cloud along until it cascaded like a waterfall down the steep side of the mountain. There was a moment's pause on this pinnacle, just time enough for us to jump back onto the runners before the dogs and sleds began to hurtle straight down the same escarpment at 30 kph towards the valley floor – where the Arctic unleashed its venom on us and we were drawn into a ground storm.

I was totally unprepared for this rapid change in weather. Had my escapade with my jacket on the Charity Challenge the previous year been training for today? Then, we had been sledding along the trail as it gradually got colder and colder and what we thought was the start of a storm began with freezing rain. For that challenge we had been issued with Arctic suites, not salopettes and jackets as this year. I had been getting very chilly and my Arctic suit was not sufficient protection from the rain. So, I had lent over the handle of my sled and taken off my over-mitts and stuffed them into the sled. Then I had opened my bag, taken out my jacket and had put my left arm in the sleeve – silly really as the wind had been coming from the right. It was continually blowing my jacket away, so just picture the scene: I am bent right over the handle of the sled with one arm in my jacket whilst the rest of the jacket blows well away from my right arm. Not wanting to lose touch with my sled I put the collar of my jacket into my mouth and, still holding onto the sled with my body, I had tried to get my right arm into the other sleeve. After several attempts I managed it, but the cuff of my Arctic suit was caught inside the sleeve and I was stuck leaning over the handle with my arms pinned behind my back. A concerted effort and it was on. Still leaning over the handle I had zipped it up, put on my over-mitts and regained proper control of the sled.

This had taken some considerable time and within a few minutes of my success the rain had stopped, the sun had come out again and – you've guessed it – I was then too hot. So the whole procedure had to be reversed until the jacket was folded and wedged onto the sled again. How I had managed to do the whole thing without falling off the sled I don't know but the threatened storm had just been a rain shower.

I was learning a lot more about the Arctic this time. It would lull us into a false sense of security only to punish us with blistering winds and plummeting temperatures going well below the -20°C the dogs could cope with. One minute I loved the place and the next I hated it; at this moment I was wondering why I ever agreed to come on the expedition. But perhaps I am just bewitched by the place.

When I was younger I loved the strength of the sun on my body and found it difficult to cope with freezing temperatures. Now when I have been away from it for a while, I want to get back to the cold and embark on another expedition. Lulled into that false sense of security since my arrival in Norway – it had been cold, but sunny and invigorating – it just had not occurred to me when Per Thore gave me my Arctic jacket soon after our arrival to fit it and the hood, checking how it fastened before we set out. Would I ever learn to follow the Girl Guide code and 'be prepared'? Consequently, the only protection I had from this piercingly freezing wind from the ground storm was a flapping jacket and an ill-fitting hood. Whilst I frantically tried to fasten my jacket, hold onto the sled and keep the hood around my face – as well as see through my almost

Photo 16 — The Haalti mountains Photo: C. O'Dowd

opaque sunglasses – the wind was still blowing ferociously across the valley floor. Cathy posted the following photo on the website, which just said it all.

The wind was too strong to be able to sort out the jacket. It was bitterly cold and I just could not do it all at the same time. With no protection afforded from my hood against such a strong wind, I could feel the icy coldness creeping down my neck and steadily chilling my body, making me curse my stupidity in not being better prepared. The ground storm was bad enough with Per Thore, who was directly in front of me, appearing and disappearing like a ghostly figure. At times I completely lost sight of him and the swirling snow was rapidly increasing and freezing on the inside of my sunglasses and threatening to block even the faintest glimmer of light. Even our thick-coated huskies who fared best in -10°C to -20°C were huddling together as they tried to run turning their backs to the wind – the temperature was now -30°C and falling. It took my mind back to Soppero and the white-out when we had not been allowed to sled for fear of frostbite and fatalities.

Of course, Per Thore was used to this weather and was well prepared with his jacket and hood performing well. Cathy, who was also used to snow and storms on mountains, had also taken the time to prepare for all eventualities. So I was the only one frantically trying to rectify the situation in the middle of a ground storm. I felt so stupid. I *was* so stupid. The wind was just too strong and more and more ice was creeping unabated down my neck. I just wanted to be out of this predicament without a complete loss of face.

We could hardly move now and certainly could not see as we gradually ground to a halt. Here was a chance to sort myself out before I froze. I fumbled with the jacket but the snow-laden sunglasses were a definite disadvantage. It was unbelievably, bitterly, bitterly cold and suddenly, out of the swirling ground storm there was Cathy lying on the ground in front of my dogs filming. Oh no, I thought please not this – let's get moving. This is hell on earth standing still in this bitterly freezing wind. I couldn't believe it. I knew we wanted to make a good film but survival was the name of the game at this point. However, stay we did. I dug my ice anchor in, raced to Per Thore and asked him if he could help me to sort out my hood (it was impossible to do on my own in these conditions). I duly received my first reprimand for being unprepared in the line of battle. It was one of those times again when I felt really foolish at not thinking through every eventuality – would I ever learn? This was becoming a repeated refrain.

Just as suddenly, Cathy was gone and we were off again. But I felt really depressed – was this what it was going to be like all the way along? Were we going to have to sacrifice the ethos of the expedition to make the documentary? Now I understood why David had disappeared into the ether as soon as filming the expedition had been mentioned. He had also raised money dog-sledding for Cancer Research UK with Per Thore the year before, but, unlike me, had always been keen to do more. As soon as I told him we would be filming, his enthusiasm had waned and eventually he had reluctantly pulled out. Writing a book is a different matter. I didn't stop to make notes but tried to remember everything until all was done for the day and I was safely ensconced in my sleeping bag to write it all up. But it was becoming difficult to write propped up with nothing to lean on and I was so tired after sledding for hours and hours and then doing the chores: my notes were getting very sketchy. So I resorted to taking lots of photos, being very careful not to replicate my actions of the previous year. Back then, I made a near-fatal mistake. Not long after we set off, we went down a very long slope onto the lake. Per Thore had stopped for what seemed like ages to ensure everyone had made it safely down the slope, so I decided it was a good opportunity to take a photograph as we were in a very picturesque area. But just as I was taking it, Per Thore had decided to move off and, with my over-mitts on, I hadn't been able to put my camera away. I had let go of the sled for just a moment and the dogs had been off – and so was I, but not with them. I hadn't fallen but I hadn't been able to catch them in time. Luckily for me, Taisto had been standing by his snowmobile just making sure that we had all managed to get down the slope and onto the lake without difficulty. He had jumped over Moira's dogs and had caught mine. Thanking him I had said 'That was lucky' to which he had responded pointedly 'You almost killed yourself then'. I was not quite sure how I would have done that; but I had made a mental note, I certainly wasn't going to do it again.

So, back to the here and now: I was also talking into a small tape recorder which I carried in my pocket. This seemed to work and on my return I had my journal, my tapes, the photos (although a lot of them looked remarkably the same), a map of the route and my memories.

By now, Cathy had managed to change from sunglasses to goggles but I was still struggling with a ground storm and sunglasses – not by choice but due to a lack of time. I had to get the glasses off and search in the tightly packed rucksack for my goggles. Maybe having a larger rucksack was the answer – more room to find what you needed and be able to do it quickly. I must have looked really odd – at least Cathy couldn't take a photograph of me at this particular moment. Eventually, defeated, I had to ask Per Thore to stop again so that I could relinquish my sunglasses and change to my goggles. Above us was blue sky and I could still see the sun shining; but at ground level I could hardly make out Per Thore's dogs and could only see the top half of him. We just had to weather the storm. This was time for a short-term goal – to get away from the ground storm as quickly as we could. We were sledding parallel with the mountain and desperately needed to get to the end of the valley to get out of the storm. This meant weaving in and out of rocky outcrops, sometimes even going straight over the top with the dogs' paws skittering as they tried to get a grip on the icy rocks. It was extremely unnerving but by now I was beginning to wonder whether in these conditions I might get frost-nip as the wind was so cold, it was stinging my face and numbing it. In fact, ice was beginning to form on my face. My hands were so cold that I had pulled on my mittens over my waterproof gloves.

My dogs loved to follow Per Thore but would turn a little earlier than he had done – I hadn't quite mastered the art of steering this unwieldy sled and consequently I often met a lump of rock that he had negotiated. No matter how far I leant out I still could not avoid it. Over I went again. The weight of our sleds made them very difficult to pick up. I weigh just 60 kilos so it was almost impossible for me to pick up the sled on my own. Cathy came to my rescue, but by now Per Thore was a long way ahead. As we managed to get the sled upright again the dogs were off, despite the ice anchor being in, Cathy hung on and I quickly jumped on. Once I was secure she jumped off and went back to her dogs – this was the ultimate in teamwork. As we traversed these rocky outcrops, Per Thore would suddenly disappear over what looked like the edge of a cliff and you just had to follow into the abyss – it was a real leap of faith. We had just traversed the Haalti mountains; as we left the valley

I turned to look back to see these fantastically majestic mountains with their own tablecloth of snowdrift, reminiscent of Table Mountain in South Africa. It had been a nightmare going through the valley; but now we were clear, it was certainly beautiful to behold the source of all our problems.

Photo 17 – Ice-blue melting lakes (see page 119)

As we left the rocky outcrops behind us we came to a series of frozen lakes where the dogs and sled slid uncontrollably across the ice. The wind was so strong that it blew the sleds out of line and the dogs' paws would skitter across the surface; so as soon as we came to a long firm surface, it was a real relief to both humans and dogs to be able to sled properly. This was the day that we seemed to have been going uphill most of the time and the dogs had worked so hard for us. They were continually working, working, working pulling the sleds and us along as we mushed or ran and pushed the sleds up the hill trying to help them as much as we could. They just couldn't get such a heavy load to the top on their own. Once we got to the top, the trail on the other side would be virtually straight down. The dogs loved it and would run like mad; but again, the sled would go faster than the dogs, requiring just the right amount of braking. You could not afford to lose concentration for a moment.

By now the dogs were very tired. They'd had to work really hard in temperatures far lower than they liked; but slowly they perked up and even managed to run down a few more slopes. Per Thore was way off ahead and Cathy way behind so it was just me, the dogs, the scenery and silence again. The sun was out, the sky was blue with a scattering of cirrus clouds above and the scenery was so beautiful. It's impossible to imagine – you just had to be there, it was so amazing, absolutely amazing. A different world. These were the moments when everything was exactly as I had dreamed it. It was romantic and momentarily allowed me to think my own thoughts and revel in the surroundings. The sun created the most incredible shadows on the mountain – sometimes they were light and dark, in various hues of blue and grey; at another they were the brownish-black of the stone. The sky was an intense blue with changing cloud patterns. On one side were rounded mountains and to the other side the mountains were mainly exposed rock where the wind had whisked the snow away.

We made our way to the summit only to find another steep downwards slope with Per Thore heading up the other side. There were always more and more mountains but each looked different with the shadows of the clouds racing across the plateau as the dogs whisked us across it. We were approaching Reisa National Park.

Eventually we came out onto a carpet of white as far as the eye could see. We sled on and on and gradually in the distance we could make out a dark speck. We circled round what was obviously a frozen lake and, as we drew nearer, rising out of the deep snow was a tiny cabin half hidden by the very large volume of snow on its roof. On and on round the lake we sled until there in front of us was the Somas cabin – even close to it was still half-hidden in the snow. This was our home for the night. It was bitterly, bitterly cold. Cathy and I unharnessed the dogs and it was obvious that the only place we were going to find water was from the frozen lake. We unloaded my sled into the cabin, which meant carrying heavy plastic boxes down a solid slippery slope of ice before stepping into the cabin, all muscles tensed to try and avoid that hard, undignified landing on your backside spraying the contents of each box across the ice.

Meanwhile, Per Thore unloaded some of his sled so that he could take it back to the lake to search for water and carry the water back up to the cabin in the insulated bags. However, as he set off, one of his lead dogs should have gone right at his command but decided it would go left so he stopped the sled, went up to the lead dog and pushed it down, knelt on it and growled at it. When he got back on the sled and gave the command to go right it obeyed. I was shocked, how could he be so cruel? I had always thought he loved all animals especially his dogs but when I mentioned this to him later he explained that this was the way you disciplined them. You had to be top dog – literally.

The cabin was not nearly as warm as the one the previous night but, having unpacked the sled, Cathy and I took a moment to grab a lunchtime sandwich. Meanwhile, Per Thore was having trouble finding water – he struck lucky with the second attempt; on his first attempt at drilling he had struck the

Photo 18 – Somas cabin, half hidden in the snow

beach. Having loaded up his sled with the insulating bags full of water, he eventually returned to the cabin and he and I set about preparing the dogs' food. Once that was on the go we went inside to start our meal and then, whilst it was cooking, Per Thore and I went outside again to feed the dogs. In the evenings Cathy usually got engrossed dealing with the technical equipment and updating the website. Her dispatch on this occasion read:

550 km to go...

69° 17' N, 21° 30' E Somas Cabin. Day 3: we covered 48 km, at an average speed of 16.3 km/h. The speedometer topped out at 25 km/h. So far we have travelled 109 km – 550 to go!

Cathy: Today started out beautifully, with blue skies and smooth untracked snow glittering in the sunlight. The only sign of life was the tracks of an Arctic fox. And running behind us the single sinuous line of our sled tracks and paw prints.

However, having crossed a high plateau, we found ourselves in the teeth of the wind. A ground storm whipped up, with spindrift scudding along the snow. Hoods wrapped round our faces, we pressed on, sleds being pushed sideways by the gusts, dogs trotting with heads tucked in.

In the bitter cold fingers and noses were going numb. Rona and Per Thore were only visible from the waist-up, their dogs vanished in the spindrift.

For a while we followed a river-course, the dogs' paws skittering on the blue ice. And finally we approached the Reisa National Park, running along a hard-packed snowmobile trail. The only breaks all day were to lift fallen sleds (today Rona's, not mine), untangle dogs from each other and once from a hidden fence, and once to gulp down luke-warm tea from thermoses while huddled down beside our sleds.

We were glad to finally reach the cabin.

When all the dogs had been fed we went back inside and Per Thore finished making the meal which we consumed in minutes. Then we left Cathy to do the washing up before she returned to the technical side of things. It wasn't long before we all turned in for the night – it had been another long, hard day. We had covered 48 kilometres at an average speed of 10.3 kph but with a top speed of 25 kph.

But, as ever, there is one last thing to do before you creep inside your sleeping bag to rest those weary bones; and this last effort is made in the hope that you will save yourself the trouble of having to crawl out of your sleeping bag in the middle of the night and take a walk in the dark across the slippery slopes to relieve yourself. Per Thore was very insistent that we should not try to resist the call of nature. He explained it would sap our energy trying to keep any waste products warm. When we had been on the Charity Challenge we had always stayed in cabins which were obviously built with tourists in mind. Whilst there was no running water or electricity, a little farther away from the main cabin was a much smaller building. It was very small. Each side was the width of the door and inside there was a plank of wood suspended from one side to the other with a hole in it about 30 cms or so across. This was the toilet. Often it would have a slated roof with gaps so the snow would creep inside and land on the plank so your bottom was in great danger of freezing onto the plank.

However, this expedition was very different. So off I went in the hope that I would be able to sleep through till morning. Sometimes we try to fool ourselves even when we know we are aiming for the impossible.

CHAPTER 5

Halfway House

So while we are at this point of the day, let's deal with a subject which cannot be ignored. It is part of our everyday life; but when you are doing things that are not 'everyday', something has to change. You are in the wilderness surrounded by a desert of snow and mountains, you have none of the normal basic equipment to hand, nor do you have the luxury or the space to take with you the amount of underwear that you would normally use over a two- to three-week period. OK, so how are you going to deal with personal hygiene? Well, on the 1996 BT Global Challenge Round-the-World Yacht Race they were in exactly the same position, and several of the crews decided that men and women alike would use panty-liners. I thought if they can do it, why not I? So I decided panty-liners it would be.

Now there is something quite difficult about waking up in the morning, putting on more layers of thermals together with your boots, jacket and hat and crawling out of a tent to find a secluded spot so that you can take down your salopettes, reveal your backside to a howling gale in -4ºC and go to the toilet. It doesn't help if you also have to put on a fresh panty-liner which won't stick to the gusset of your knickers because the temperature is so low. The wind catches it and blows it away leaving you with only one option which is to waddle, with your knickers down round your ankles, over to where it landed to try to catch it before it flies further into the wilderness. If you are lucky first time around, give yourself a cheer. There is a fine art involved here that is not covered in the basic training. To preserve your modesty you waddle back to the favoured spot with said panty-liner, show it who is boss, making sure it goes where it's meant to go, so that you can restore your modesty and return to your tent for breakfast. It is not the easiest start to any day.

Once all the breakfast was cleared away and everything packed, we loaded the sleds and harnessed the dogs as usual. The intelligent and usually slightly smaller dogs were harnessed at the front and would lead the other dogs. The bigger and stronger dogs were harnessed nearer the sled – or as Cathy called them, the 'dumb brutes' – as these were the ones who would get the sled moving. We were just about to set off when out of nowhere, in the distance, there appeared a cross-country skier pulling his pulka.

We stood there watching, totally bemused. Where had he come from and where was he going? We will never know – he was far too far away for us to start a conversation and anyway, our words would have been whisked off by the wind. We watched him pass by before resuming our own preparations. In a flash we were off down the hill racing towards the lake, retracing some of the previous day's journey. Per Thore went first as usual, then Cathy and then me. Only this time we did not circle the lake as we had done the night before, we went straight across it.

Cathy's dispatch that day was a picture with the caption:

Vinga and Sally leading Rona's team of eight dogs out of Reisa National Park.

Photo 19 – Leaving Reisa National Park (see page 119)

As we sled over this white plateau I indulged in my usual practice of looking back at where we had come from and all I could see were the curved mounds of the mountains with the clouds throwing dark shadows on them. There was nothing but the shadows, the tracks of our sleds and the paw prints of 26 dogs as we raced towards a small ridge. Still the only noise we could hear was the swish of the runners on the snow, the 'ha ha ha' panting of the dogs as they pulled our heavy sleds, aided and abetted by us, and the pitter patter, pitter patter of their paws. It was spectacular, the colour of the ice-covered snow modulating between greys and blues, reflecting the clouds, and the long dark shadows changing as we sled farther along. Looking back all I could see was the sun still making wonderful shadows on the mountains where the occasional black rock dramatically cut through the snow, a cloudless blue sky and only our trail winding its way down towards us – there was nothing else. Apart from that solitary skier we were totally alone in this silent white wilderness. Then we started climbing. I could see nothing ahead of us except this ridge. Above us was the blue sky but to our right, on the edge of the plateau, you could see just the faint wisps of the clouds hanging in the valley below and, as we sled along, these clouds slowly started to rise out of the valley as the sun gently warmed the air.

Suddenly, it was as though we were racing towards the edge of the world. Beyond the edge of the plateau in front of us was a cloud clinging to the edge of this abyss. It grew gradually darker as we sled onward; we were in shadow and the temperature plummeted. We were getting closer and closer to the ridge when Per Thore suddenly disappeared from sight as he sled over the precipice into the abyss and there was no trace of him at all. First Per Thore disappeared

Photo 20 — Into the abyss

then Cathy and then the sun disappeared completely as we were enveloped by the cloud. Once over the edge we started to rapidly descend the other side.

As we swept down the rocky side of the mountain into the valley, bouncing and jerking our way over the jagged rocks, the sleds reacted like bucking broncos. Once out of the cloud all I could see ahead of me was the deep, deep blue of distant land. We were descending towards the tree line again. Up and down, always up and down. We sled along, gradually climbing once again to where the reindeer fences were. What I really wanted to see now were the reindeer. This was tremendous sledding, a world away from last year in Lapland. It was the real thing. Although you were physically with people, you were also strangely by yourself on your own sled with your own thoughts and your own feelings. You could let your mind wander but you always knew you had companions with you so you never really felt totally isolated – it was a very odd sensation.

Suddenly I felt saddened that my fellow sledders from the Charity Challenge had decided not to join us. This was what they had wanted to do by the time we arrived at the end of that trail but each one had found a reason (or was it an excuse?) not to participate. Had other challenges taken its place or family or work commitments taken precedence? Was that exuberance of wanting to face a more demanding challenge just the exuberance of having accomplished a goal? Or was it just a dream which was never to be fulfilled?

We were now bouncing down another mountain where there were lots of rocky outcrops slowly melting away into lines of stubby little trees. This whole area resembled sand dunes blanketed in snow, and every so often we could see the paw marks of an Arctic fox. This was the time of year when the Sámi people move the herds of reindeer from the lower winter pastures up to the mountains for the summer. The previous year when we had the white out, we had stopped at Soppero where Per Thore's friends Per Nils and Brit Marie had a large house to accommodate sledders and a museum showing how the Sámi people lived their nomadic life looking after the reindeer. In fact, as we were caught in the storm and had to stay there longer than anticipated, they both came in their traditional Sámi outfits made entirely of reindeer skins. Brit Marie gave us a tour of their museum explaining how they lived at one with the environment and the reindeer. It was fascinating.

But now we had more constraints on us. The reindeer were carrying calves and could be easily frightened by the dogs. We were now descending the mountain towards the Njallaavi valley and Per Thore saw reindeer on the opposite side ready to be moved through the valley. Stopping us, he pointed out that there were reindeer ahead so no matter what happened we mustn't let go of the sleds – had I heard that somewhere before? If the reindeer passed near us then we had to keep the dogs still and quiet so Per Thore instructed us, if necessary, to be quite harsh with them. We had to be quick and quiet because disturbing the reindeer would cause mayhem. The route took us into the valley where we had to navigate up and down steep little hills, twisting and turning round obstacles and trees. Later that night, in the security of our tent, Cathy and I nicknamed it the Roller Coaster Valley. It is all very well saying that you have to go quickly when the trail is hard but the weather conditions had made some parts of the trail soft, and there were hidden ruts as the snow had gradually started to thaw.

As leader and navigator Per Thore would go first; Cathy and I would try to take it in turns to go second or third. It all depended on the position of your sled when you harnessed the dogs in the morning, or when you stopped for a moment's respite, as well as whose dogs were more rested. Whoever went second, their dogs seemed to keep up with Per Thore but, if you were third, the dogs would gradually drop farther and farther behind. The previous year, in preparation for the Charity Challenge, I had trained for upper-body strength and had found it quite difficult to run up the mountains pushing the sled even though it had been quite light; so this time I had concentrated on lower body strength (so that I could run behind the sled pushing it up the mountains helping the dogs.) However, now each sled weighed 120 kilos but I weighed only 60. What I did not realise was that this time I would have to be continually trying to lift twice my body weight. I resolved that in future, no matter what the expedition was, I would train my whole body so that I covered all eventualities.

On this particular day Cathy was third. It was really hard work going through the Roller Coaster Valley because as soon as you leant one way to get round a bend, you had to quickly lean over the other way to get round the next bend in the opposite direction. We were also going up over the top of these dunes made of snow and down the other side. It was like a crazy white-knuckle ride. No wonder there were accidents and we both fell off – as usual, Per Thore just sled on. At times he reminded me a little of the dogs; when he occasionally stopped to wait for us he'd turn back and he would have the same look in his eyes as they did which I would interpret as 'Oh no, they have fallen again'. I often wondered what he was really thinking. The snow was soft and deep but, try as I might, I could not always keep to Per Thore's tracks. The sleds made deep ruts as they went through this particular valley, which increased the danger of them tipping over if you weren't quite quick enough to lean in the right direction at precisely the right time and keep the dogs going as well. As we entered the valley Per Thore wasted no time. He wanted to get through and out the other side as quickly as possible as the reindeer were only 100 metres away.

Well, they say pride comes before a fall. We had been careering through the valley and I was silently congratulating myself on still being upright and in contact with the sled as we raced down a hill and round a left-hand bend. A left-handed bend means that you have to hang over to the left, otherwise the sled will topple to the right; but just past the bend on the left-hand side there was a deep rut and my left runner was heading straight for it. I had gone round the corner flat out, leaning over to stop the sled tipping, but now found that my left-hand runner was actually in mid-air – I flung myself to the right. Anyone who knows anything at all about physics will know that eight dogs pulling one way followed by a 120-kilo sled with one runner in mid-air over a rut and one 60-kilo body flinging itself to the right to counterbalance the sled will result in disaster. The sled went over into the rut, this time more than 90° – I really was too light – and as much as I tried there was no way that I could lift it upright again.

Eventually Cathy appeared round the corner coming to my rescue and between us we man-handled the sled into the upright position. But as soon as the pressure was released the dogs were off and as I was standing with both legs thigh deep in snow it was just impossible for me to 'jump' onto the runners in time. I wonder why? With so much soft snow and no-one in control the sled tipped over again in a matter of metres. With a resigned look at each other, Cathy and I trudged up the trail to the sled and picked it up yet again; but this time Cathy held it and I had a chance to extract my legs from their thigh-deep prison of snow and jump onto the runners. Success – with dogs and human working together, we managed to stay upright. But then we had

67

Photo 21 – Oops, now that's a first – that's Per Thore's sled

a 'first'. Ahead we saw that Per Thore's sled had just gone over. He had been looking at the maps when one runner went into a deep rut and over it went.

We were just quick enough to get a photograph – there would be one or two people back in the UK who would love to see a copy of that! When I had been on the Charity Challenge he hadn't put a foot wrong whilst we volunteers had been struggling to get even a reasonable level of co-ordination – and back then, the sleds only weighed 15 kilos.

Altogether once more, we continued on through the valley and gradually started to climb up the Muvasto mountains on the other side. On and on we went, gradually going higher and higher, still twisting and turning round trees but now, somehow, the going seemed to be a little easier. Soon we were back sledding across a wide open plateau and to our right at regular intervals were thick posts. These were the posts for the fence that the Sámi people would erect, once the reindeer had gone through on their way up the mountains, to stop them going back down to the pastures in the valley. This would give the valley grass a chance to rejuvenate before the reindeer returned in time for the next winter.

Photo 22 – Lunch by the reindeer fence (see page 120)

We had lunch by a gap in the reindeer fence but we didn't stop for long: in fact, we ate lunch standing on the sled runners. Our trail had been running parallel to the posts but now we turned and passed through the fence poles, away from the valley. Up to the right-hand side, high on the mountainside, I could see another large herd of reindeer on its way towards the mountains near the coast. Whenever possible, Cathy and I were taking photographs of the scenery, of each other, in fact, of any incident that we thought might be interesting.

On and on we sled. We were definitely getting tired now, having set off that morning at 9.15 a.m. The extreme cold and the physical exercise takes a lot out of you especially when you couple it with all the weight-lifting we were doing to get the sleds upright. We passed some Sámi people on snowmobiles carrying lots of fencing on a trailer ready to erect the fence as soon as the reindeer had been driven through and now we were beginning to wonder where our destination was for the night. There was no alternative but to keep on going only now, thank goodness, at a slightly more moderate pace. We sled on and on with the distance between us lengthening and lengthening. Whenever Per Thore stopped to look at the map it was our chance to catch up with him.

We came down a steep slope twisting and turning through the trees, then dashed across a road coming face to face with some loose dogs. Despite a considerable amount of barking, luckily, our dogs just ignored them and we

Photo 23 — Rona getting odder by the day — the trail taking its toll
Photo: C. O'Dowd

turned round a bend and went hell for leather back down another steep slope to find ourselves on yet another frozen river. This one was called the Kautokeino River. It was very long and very windy and was to prove to be a challenge for both man and beast – and very nearly our undoing.

Now maybe I should explain more about this land we were exploring. Whilst large tracts of this fascinating Arctic terrain are never-ending rolling blankets of snow with not a sign of civilisation for kilometre upon kilometre, I was surprised when we would suddenly happen upon a hamlet with no visible means of access. It is a land where roads cling to the coastline never venturing inland, to what we, who usually live nearer the 51° parallel, would consider to be a hostile environment, except very occasionally when part of the road will branch off to explore a path inland towards a foreign border, making a rare lifeline for the inhabitants. Even more occasionally, one of these roads would cross our path. A sled with eight dogs is a long and unwieldy vehicle but there is a lot of camaraderie amongst the dogs so if one sled takes the route across a road the others will follow, regardless of what danger may be hurtling towards them. Maybe this was the reason the Norwegians thought we 'gals' were too inexperienced to succeed, as stopping the dogs, for me, was a nightmare – I was just not heavy enough. It's not often we 'gals' wish we were heavier!

It was getting late but the going was easier now as we sled along the flat frozen river. Suddenly, Per Thore turned abruptly to the left, went over a snow bridge with open water either side and up a near-vertical bank where some frozen grass was exposed. Turning left again he came to a halt high up on the bank. This sloping river bank was to become our home for the night. It had

Photo 24 – Safely on the bank of the Kautokeino River

been terrifying following Per Thore as our dogs often cut the corners to get closer to him and at one point we were all clambering to get up the bank at the same time. But now we were all safely on the bank away from the frozen river and where the snow was deep and soft, making moving very difficult. To add a degree of difficulty, as if we hadn't enough to contend with, it sloped away in all directions. I wondered why it was that wherever the chains were strung out for the dogs at the end of the day always happened to be where the snow was deepest and softest so that I was up to my thighs in snow as I took each step. I suppose it did make it nicer for the dogs.

We would unharness two dogs at a time. Trying to hold two dogs, who amazingly still had some running left in them, and walk thigh-deep in snow and then harness them onto the chain was a feat that I found extremely challenging. Once the dogs were unharnessed, Per Thore would immediately start to cut up the reindeer meat. However, this time we did not have to drill a hole to get water as the edge of the river was beginning to melt so we could just scoop it up from there – a bonus after a long and difficult day. Once the dogs were fed we could pitch the tent on what, that night, turned out to be a very bumpy site. Now there was a chance to relax a little whilst cooking and eating our evening meal. It was whilst we were all eating that I voiced the fear that would not go out of my mind – how to get back onto the frozen river in the morning? Per Thore just calmly told me not to worry and Cathy said 'Just go for it, Rona'. So there was a lot of sympathy to be had from those two! In fact, when I mentioned it again after Per Thore had left, Cathy just said the same thing again. Didn't anyone realise how scared I was? We settled down to sleep but, no matter what I did, I could not get rid of a small mound of snow that dug into my back all night long – that was, when I wasn't slipping down the hill into the bottom of my sleeping bag. It was a most uncomfortable night although exhaustion took over and I did eventually manage to get some sleep.

At least I was warm, which I certainly hadn't been the first night we camped. We had been very tired when we had arrived at this site at 7 p.m. having been sledding for ten hours – covering 90 kilometres with a top speed of 18 kph – and having had only a very short break for lunch. Cathy's dispatch for the website read:

A big day

76° 55' N 22° 36' E Addgetgekke.

Average speed 10.4 km/h. Covered 90 km in nine hours of sledding, done 199 km in total, nearly a third of the way.

A big day, crossing a lot of ground, at times in poor conditions. Temperatures are surprisingly high (relatively), the dogs are hot and the snow is soft, with the sleds tipping and jamming frustratingly easily.

Our first encounters with wildlife, flocks of white birds and, on a distant skyline, herds of hundreds of reindeer.

However, there was one thing that continually preyed on my mind and that was 'what goes up must come down'. We had come up the bank, so in the morning we would have to go back down. I could see some sleds tipping over and the possibility of a dousing in the river – and there was a strong likelihood that it would be my sled.

The morning dawned and by now I was extremely apprehensive about how we would leave the bank to get back down onto the frozen river. We went about our chores: Per Thore and I fed the dogs as usual and cleared everything up – including the dogs' excrement which had to be carried away on the sleds. Thank goodness my sled was kept for human food and equipment only.

Having packed my sled I then helped Cathy to demolish our tent. Earlier I had taken a few minutes out and, feeling a little like a jockey at the start of a big race (the Grand National sprang to mind), had walked down to the first 'jump' – the bank. It is amazing just how your imagination can get something you are concerned about so out of proportion overnight. When I looked at where we were coming from and where we had to go, the bank did not look nearly so steep. Don't get me wrong, it was still steep and would need some careful navigation but not nearly as steep as I'd remembered it. However, the snow bridge was still an issue. I stood looking at it for a few minutes trying to work out how I would deal with it, half hoping that Per Thore would either take the sleds down or help us to do it. What a wimp! Who was I kidding? Per Thore had great faith in our being capable of accomplishing this little exercise, otherwise we would not be on the expedition.

Now it was time to harness the dogs in readiness for another day's sledding. I'm not sure how it happened but in positioning my sled so that my dogs did not get tangled with Cathy's, mine was slightly in front of hers and to the left of our little 'train' with the river on our right. Once the dogs were harnessed and with everything packed and all dog 'dirt' collected, we were ready to go. I found it somewhat disconcerting to find that Per Thore was at the back and made no effort whatsoever to come forward to help us through this tricky manoeuvre.

Little did we realise just how eventful our start would be that Thursday morning. 'OK Rona, off you go' called Per Thore. Well, there was nothing for it – I shouted at the dogs to go and leaned well over to the left making the sled slew round so that the back was further left but the front was beginning to point towards the snow bridge on the right. Then just as my lead dog Vinga was nearly past the snow bridge, I shouted 'Vinga Herra' and threw my body to the right to counterbalance the sled. 'Herra' is a shortened version of 'right' in Norwegian, but the fact that it sounds different from left ('Vance') means that the dogs understand. Now what you need to know here is that if the dogs don't trust you they will not do what you ask of them. I needn't have worried: like a well-oiled machine, Vinga turned to her right taking the other dogs, the sled and me straight down the bank over the snow bridge and onto the frozen river. It was exhilarating. Not only had I not fallen into the river – famous last words – but my dogs had obeyed me.

I brought the sled to a halt, albeit now facing in the direction we had come from the night before and not the direction we wanted to go, put the ice-anchor in and turned to see how the others were getting on. As I did, Cathy was coming down the slope towards the point where her dogs needed to turn sharply to the right, but the dogs have a habit of cutting corners and I stared in amazement as they turned and came down the slope over the snow bridge and onto the river. Whether Cathy had not been able to manoeuvre or whether it hadn't worked, her sled was heading not for the snow bridge but for the open water to the right of it. She jumped off onto the snow bridge and just stared at the sled which for the briefest of moments floated on top of the water. As usual the dogs were raring to go so continued to pull preventing the sled from sinking too far. However, as the sled took on more and more water, Cathy watched as it slowly started to sink. The dogs were being pulled backwards towards the open water. Valiantly, they tried hard to go forward digging their claws into the frozen river surface as hard as they could. It was a challenge they were likely to lose as the slightly pointed front of the sled was caught under the ice. I jumped off my sled and raced back to the other side of the open water to try to lift the sled, which was not only sinking but tipping over to the right as well, back onto the ice and upright again. Only now I was on thin ice – literally. I tried to reach the sled but it was deep and heavy and, just as I caught it, and started to lift it the weight went through my body and put pressure on the thawing ice beneath me. It gave way and I slipped into the water. I quickly lay back on the ice and rolled out. Luckily I had only got wet up to my knees. Sometimes watching survival programmes can be very useful. Thank you, Ray Mears!

All this time Cathy was just standing immobile on the snow bridge as though in a complete daze contemplating the scenario. She didn't move – nor did she make any effort to try to help me, and Per Thore was still stuck up on the bank unable to move as Cathy was blocking his way. I shouted at Cathy to move so that Per Thore could come racing down and, with no mishap at all, he arrived on the frozen river. Meanwhile Cathy's dogs were straining against

Photo 25 — The end of the video?

the weight of not only a very heavy sled but one which was fast becoming waterlogged. Slowly they were being pulled backwards towards the water. Braking hard and digging his ice anchor in, Per Thore called to me to stand on his brake. Our dogs wouldn't go past him but if his dogs went we would be in trouble. I jumped on the brake with both feet and before you could blink an eye he'd got hold of the front of Cathy's sled and, with one movement, pulled it free of the water. Without any fuss or bother he immediately started to undo the waterproof cover and remove everything from Cathy's sled, handing all technical equipment to her to deal with whilst he emptied the water, wrung out clothes and cleared and dried the sled as best he could.

This was all done in complete silence. All the technical equipment belonged to Cathy and so it was kept in her sled. Despite having bought zip-lock bags the night before we left England, Cathy had put her clothes in them and none of the technical equipment had been protected from this sort of predicament at all. There was a strong possibility that it would all be beyond repair. However, it was not over yet: just at that moment my dogs decided to move off – and in the wrong direction – so Per Thore raced after them and brought them back. Once Cathy's sled was repacked with all the waterlogged equipment resting on the top in the hope that it would dry out in the sunshine and be useable again, we sled off along the river. If we could not dry out the video camera then there would be no documentary to sell at the end of the expedition, an important part of Cathy's plan.

The accident had put a bit of a damper on the day to say the least. However, this was the day a UK radio station wanted a live interview with me and for this we would need to use the satellite phone. We had been sledding for a while when Per Thore stopped in the middle of the river. As we drew up behind him he told us to put our ice anchors in as we were going to rest for a while as it was too hot for the dogs – the temperature had risen to a heady -4ºC. He told us not to forget to change our socks which were now soaking wet. So Cathy and I chatted for a little while and then returned to our sleds. I took the opportunity of leaning against the sled and writing a few more notes as an *aide de memoire* for the writing of this book.

As I wrote down what had happened, my mind went back to the incident of the previous year when we had arrived at Esrange and a series of accidents had put an end to another film opportunity. It was like déjà vu. We had been doing some crazy sledding over a vast lake. By 'crazy', I mean extremely fast; but then we had swished round a right-angled bend, up a small hill and through the trees. Suddenly, there in front of me, had been a ridge of snow with a building behind it. My dogs had been determined to go over it and I had been determined to go around it – result? The dogs had won and the sled and I had fallen to the ground – this scenario had been getting tedious. I had started to get up, the dogs had realised and had started to run so I had quickly gone down – I had needed a little more time. Trying to catch them unawares I had got up again quickly but had held the sled down until the last minute when I had jumped onto the runners and had just about made it round the corner without hitting a very large tree only to find that (in fact) we had arrived at our destination for that night.

The lodge where we would cook, eat and sleep had been tiny for the twelve of us but luckily there was a separate cabin for Sid, Digger and Per Thore, although they would join us to eat. Towards the lake there had been a very smart-looking cabin which housed a very hot sauna. (On the Nordkapp there would be no sauna until we eventually arrived at the half-way house.) Whilst the toilet building was behind our lodge and further into the woods, it had two toilets – a real bonus. The seats had been made of polystyrene – more comfortable and just a little warmer for our posteriors; in fact, pure luxury. Behind the cabin was the boiler house which had held the reindeer meat for the dogs and, of course, the boiler to boil the water to prepare the soup. If you had retraced our trail down the hill passed the sauna and then continued on down the steep slope to the edge of the frozen lake and kept on walking, you would have come to a pole in the ice. This denoted an ice-hole from which we had had to ladle buckets and buckets of water for the dogs and for ourselves. It was drinkable although it had a very peaty taste.

Photo 26 – Rona testing the water (see page 120)

The assigned duty for our group then had been dog patrol. We had fed the dogs – well, when I say 'we' there had been about five of us to begin with fetching water for the boiler from the ice-hole and carrying it up the hill through the forest to the boiler time and time again whilst Per Thore had rhythmically swung the axe, thud, thud, thud, over and over again to chop enough frozen meat to make the soup for 70 dogs. But it had taken quite a long time for the water for the soup for 70 dogs to boil and my fellow 'dog patrol' sledders had decided that there had not been enough to keep them occupied so had disappeared. Once all was prepared, I had put out the dog bowls and had started to ladle the soup into them, then I collected the empty bowls and moved them on to the next set of hungry dogs, ladling out more soup for them. At one point, Per Thore had come out of his cabin and had asked:

'Where are the rest of them?'

'I don't know.'

'So you are feeding the dogs on your own?'

'Well yes, I suppose I am.'

'Oh! I will take you on an expedition anytime.'

And with that he had come and helped me. Little did I realise at the time that within twelve months those words would become a reality. Per Thore was the kind of guy who always appreciated the fact that someone tried. The wings on my heart fluttered in excitement. Perhaps now is the time to explain that when we started off in the mornings as soon as Per Thore appeared from his cabin, all the dogs virtually stood to attention barking madly as soon as they saw him. The interesting part was that so did all the women!

Photo 27 – Cutting wood to cook the dinner (see page 121)

The temperature was -16ºC when we got up the next morning. It was pandemonium as we had packed the sleds and harnessed the dogs. It had been bad enough that we were starting off from inside the forest but now the fun would really begin as we were divided into two groups. Per Thore had decided that it would be bedlam if we had all started from inside the forest – there only had to be one person who hesitated and we would all have been tangled up together. So one group would leave Esrange along the continuation of the path that we had travelled to get to the cabins, and the other group would leave from behind the main cabin but along a different path parallel with the one we had used the previous night, although down a steep slope towards the ice-hole. They would then have to take a sharp right-angled left-hand bend to bring them round the corner to join us. Difficult enough to do at the best of times but first thing in the morning when the dogs were fresh and eager to go had looked to me like a recipe for disaster. As we stood on the back of our sleds with both feet firmly planted on the brake, the safety line had been removed from the tree and the ice anchor reinstated on the post on the sled – hook ends facing into the sled so as not to harm another dog on its way past. As soon as Per Thore had appeared from his cabin the dogs had started a frenzied barking and, as he got to his sled, untied the safety line and had removed his anchor, they had all come into line – and so had all the 'girls'. Our leader was with us and we were all determined to impress him.

Per Thore had decided that the other group should go first, led by Digger the Doc. We had watched with interest to see how it would work. Would Digger be able to get his dogs to turn left, how many spills would there be and would they make it down the steep slope without going into any of the trees? There had been a rush, a flurry, some shouts and before we had known it the sleds had come racing round the corner and Digger had brought them to an orderly halt just short of our exit. Now it was our turn to perform whilst they watched and waited. One by one we had released our brakes. Suddenly we were off. The dogs had shot off like bullets and I had been braking furiously. It was always the hardest moment of the day. As the dogs are rested and excited, we knew what was going to happen and it was a case of clinging onto the sled for dear life as the dogs hurtled after their master, Per Thore.

We had come out of the forest down another steep slope onto the frozen lake and abruptly turned sharp left before Per Thore had come to a halt having left enough room for us all to form up between him and Digger. I released the brake just as I had turned the corner – it had been difficult as the snow had been thick but I had made it. In fact most of us had made it. That was the good news. Now, Sue was in our group with the video camera. I could say that we had to stop innumerable times so that she could film the sleds as we had travelled but, in fact, she had been adroit enough to be able to film as we sled along. The number of times we had stopped for actual filming could not be counted – I think we had probably stopped more often for those of us who had found staying on the sled a feat beyond our remit.

Now there is always the exception that proves the rule and the reason I focused on Sue is because her moment had come. Sue had been near the end of our half of the 'train' and with camcorder in hand she had 'taken off' when instructed, burst out of the forest down the slope and had turned sharp left. Well, not exactly. Her dogs had turned left, her sled had made a valiant effort to turn left and Susan, with one hand on the sled and one on the camcorder, had gone straight ahead, landing on her side with the camcorder in the snow. Result – that was the end of the film. The camcorder had decided that enough was enough and this was one burial in the snow too many.

However, back to the Nordkapp. We just had to sit and wait on the Kautekeino river for the temperature to drop so that we could get going again.

Per Thore caught up with a snooze and the dogs lay on the snow and tried to cool down.

Photo 28 — Too hot to sled (see page 121)

As the evening drew on, the temperature dropped enough for us to set off again along the river; and as the appointed hour drew near, Cathy stopped the sleds and brought the satellite phone to me for the radio interview, giving me some instructions as to how to use it. I am not a technical person and I really needed her to show me how to use it (I am visual not auditory) but before I knew it she was back on her sled and off again. I called to her but there was no reply. I frantically tried to go over what she had fleetingly told me to do – which button was I meant to press? It would be interesting to see whether I could sled and be interviewed at the same time. It would be even more interesting to see whether the satellite telephone would even work.

Off we went, as today we needed to cover 70 kilometres to our next stop and we had already lost quite a lot of time waiting for the temperature to fall; luckily, the trail was to be mainly over flat terrain. However, my idea of flat and Per Thore's idea of flat are very different. In the winter the rivers became frozen highways threading their way like ribbons through valleys and round mountains, allowing those on this ancient mode of transport a new way to explore. As we sled along the winding river it was interesting to see how the local people utilised what for some would have been a problem. The frozen river had now become the highway and periodically we would come across a wooden road sign sticking high out of the ice showing the direction of various places and the distance in kilometres. When the spring arrives apparently the signs just disappear into the depths of the river only to be replaced the following year as it freezes over again.

I just about heard the satellite telephone ring; but despite trying to do all the right things, I could not answer the call. This was repeated a couple of times. I could not catch up with Cathy, nor could I get her to hear me. When we stopped some while later I explained to Cathy that the radio station's call had come through but when I had tried to answer the satellite telephone, it had not responded. After some difficulty she managed to contact them. The telephone had definitely not dried out properly. We did a pre-recorded interview so that they had at least got something they could put out over the airwaves. They wanted to come back to us again at some point. Whether that was going to be possible would depend on whether we could get the equipment to respond to the warm air.

Photo 29 — The latest in doggie footwear (see page 122)

Night after night the fluctuating temperatures would cause a thin layer of ice to form overnight on the snow, so when the dogs started in the morning it could cut into the soft skin between the pads of their paws. When this happened, as it did now to one of Per Thore's dogs, the paw had to have a bootee put on it, which was made of felt and held on with Velcro. During this unscheduled stop we even made a cup of coffee – pure luxury. Now Per Thore was one of those guys who had to be reminded to eat, otherwise he would just sled on continually if the dogs were happy; but today they needed to rest so he was happy to take the break. Again my dogs decided they were going to move off before time – I tried to dig the ice anchor into the ice more firmly but failed. If I am honest, what I really did was put the ice anchor down and stamp on it in the hope that it would help me to stop the dogs. However, my dogs were so strong that I had been having a continual struggle to get them to stop. Even with two feet on the brake, the snowmobile brake on and the heavy sled plus my weight of 60 kilos, they could easily pull me slowly, sedately along the trail. So when I stamped on the ice anchor all I achieved, unfortunately, was to break the rope; so I now fervently hoped I wouldn't need it for the rest of the day. It was always split-second timing when Per Thore decided he wanted to move off because as soon as the dogs saw he was ready they started pulling so they would lodge my ice anchor further into the ice making it even more difficult to extract.

Strangely, I seemed unable to pull a 120-kilo sled and eight eager dogs back in order to release the ice anchor. The only option was to be prepared to hang on to the anchor and pull it out at the very last second just before they started pulling in their eagerness to get going again – which didn't work. However, with coffee finished and the bootee on, we were now sledding along easily. The sky was deep blue, the sun was shining and for the first time we started to see

Photo 30 – Hostile country?

birds again – having come down from some 1,300 metres to 30 metres above sea level. It was lovely to see the odd bird flying around.

One of the most significant things about being this far north is the absence of wildlife, due to the climate's extreme hostility. However, the surroundings are beautiful and it was a delight to be able to sled through them. As for me, I was battered and bruised. My hands gripped the handle of the sled willing me to stay in contact with it and ride out the obstacles along the route. Each time I have gone sledding, Per Thore tells me to relax and not to grip the handle of the sled so tightly. I try, I really do. I would dearly love to finish sledding without the pain where I have gripped the sled as though my life depended on it. But maybe, just maybe it did! Probably I gripped so tightly because, on the Charity Challenge, we had been told not to let go of the sleds no matter what happened; so when mine had gone over after we had finally left Soppero following the white-out, I had done a superb impression of Superman as I was dragged along the trail on my stomach with the ice anchor bouncing around in front of my face. But now at the end of the day when I had to pick up the heavy food boxes out of the sled and put them inside the tent, the small of my back would really hurt – I ached, boy, did I ache. And some people think I lead a glamorous life!

But this was crisis day. The temperature had reached -4ºC and the dogs only function well when the temperature is between -20ºC and -10ºC. It was too hot for them again. They cannot sweat as their capillaries finish about six mm from the skin to enable them to withstand the cold. The only way they can cool off is to allow their long tongues to hang out and occasionally drag along the snow. The dogs were struggling and, despite stopping on the river for a couple of hours to give them a long rest whilst we ate lunch and waited for the temperature to drop, it just was not helping. Per Thore decided there was only one thing to do if we were ultimately to achieve our aim: the next day we would start early, rest for 3–4 hours midday and sled late into the evening. The day after that would be a rest day. Little did I know at the time that the latter decision was to prove to be a blessing for me.

Among all the photographs we were taking we actually missed the best – we were so astonished we all just stopped and stared open mouthed. It was the most remarkable sight. Let me explain. The previous year we had been sledding along a frozen river in a long train of sleds with forests on both banks. It had been breath taking and I, for one, had been totally immersed in the picturesque beauty of the area and my own thoughts when a message had been passed back from Per Thore that we must stop and be very quiet and under no circumstances should we let go of the sleds no matter what happened. We had had no idea why; I certainly hadn't seen anything untoward as we had been sledding. Somewhat bewildered we scoured the surroundings for the reason why. I hadn't been far behind Per Thore when I suddenly saw it, right there in front of us.

About 50 metres along the river a small herd of reindeer were timidly picking their way out of the forest, down the bank on the right-hand side of the river and had haltingly started to cross in front of us. Instinct told the reindeer we were there. They had been very wary. Were we friend of foe? They had paused, strung out across the river. They looked, raised their nostrils to sniff the air and, after a moment's reflection, hesitantly continued their journey keeping an eye on the dogs as they crossed. Once in the haven of the forest on the opposite side they bolted away through the trees.

But now we saw something really bizarre. Out of the wood on the far right-hand side of the river came a Sámi driving towards the middle of this frozen river on a snowmobile with a trailer hitched onto the back. He drove round the front of Per Thore's dogs and along our left-hand side. Sitting upright behind him on the snowmobile was a dog watching all that was going on around him; but on the trailer, lying comfortably like contented cows with their legs curled up under them, were three reindeer with large antlers and beside them, three large rolls of green wire fencing. We were so flabbergasted that they were past us before we could even think of a camera. What a shot that would have been – hey, why walk when you can ride?

Reindeer hitching a ride
Tony Huggins of Oxford Designers & Illustrators

The previous night Per Thore had calmly told us that at our stop the next night we would be able to get a hot shower so we were really excited – we had been sledding for over a week now and it had been baby-wipes all the way. However, in the morning, realising we had taken him seriously (we so wanted a shower after all the exertion of the previous few days) he confessed that, in fact, he had been ribbing us and there would be no hot showers. Now I wonder if that was why Cathy had decided that her sled should take a plunge in the river?

Eventually we left the river behind and started to climb up through the forests again. We were so far north that these forests were made up of stunted, spindly birch trees struggling to survive in this harsh landscape. The snow lay deeper here as the trail was partly sheltered by this dwarf forest. It made the route difficult for the dogs as with each step their paws sank into the deep snow which would be up to their bellies. As we ploughed our way through this forest I had to keep putting my brake down to stop the gangline going loose; but this meant that the snow gradually accumulated underneath the sled, building up more and more in front of the brake until it finally brought it to a complete standstill – the sled became impossible to move. Now I was really caught. I had Per Thore at the front telling me to release the anchor and Cathy was at the back trying to explain to him that it wasn't the brake it was just the sheer volume of compacted snow underneath the sled. I was in the middle struggling to go nowhere. I decided to ignore both of them and kicked and pushed and pulled and eventually, with a lot of help from the dogs, I managed to man-handle the sled next to Per Thore's, whereupon he tipped it over slightly (as if it was as light as a feather) and kicked away all the snow so that I could sled once more.

Why is it that we humans are so fickle? When we were going up and down these hills and mountains through the most beautiful scenery, I longed to be sledding across a plateau or through a valley but, as soon as I got my wish, I longed for the mountains. I think there's a very good reason why they say that variety is the spice of life.

And yes, there was yet another mountain to negotiate – up was good, but down I was not sure I had mastered. Maybe this is where I should admit that I am scared of snow and ice. When I was fifteen I went on a school holiday to Austria. We had been given some lessons on how to ski (but not how to stop) and then told to 'snow-plough' down the side of the mountain. When it was my turn, I set off very gingerly but the surface just made me go faster and faster – I was terrified. In fact, at the bottom, although there was a slight rise, I just kept on going when everyone else stopped. I hadn't quite mastered the art of stopping. The only way I managed to do so was to throw myself on my side. As I started to pick myself up virtually all of the front of my skis were over the edge of a precipice with a snow-plough crawling up the path about 30 feet below. It was the one and only time I have ever been skiing and I have no intention of ever going again. As Cathy would tell you, even now I am a real baby when I come upon even a small patch of ice.

Well, it may have been lightly wooded but there was certainly a lot of soft snow. It was horrendous – just so difficult that Per Thore decided on a different approach. (I suppose that's why it's called exploring.) We turned slightly to the right and then went down a very steep slope (really quite scary I thought); but

I was some way behind Per Thore and Cathy by this time, and they disappeared from view round a bend. I couldn't see what the next piece of terrain would be like and I didn't want to rush the dogs as they were tired. I came down the hill following the trail Per Thore had made, turning left at the bottom (some might call it a hairpin bend) when out of the corner of my eye I saw something sticking out of the snow to the right. It was only just showing above the snow and was quite small. This was one of those moments when that little thought goes fleetingly across your mind 'Oh-oh' and despite the fact that I was hanging to the left and braking for all I was worth – CRASH.

Photo 31 – Rona's downhill (see page 123)

My sled skewed to the right and stopped abruptly. There I was, firmly stuck courtesy of I knew not what. The noise of my dogs' howling alerted Per Thore to the fact that I had another calamity on my hands. The dogs turned to look at me, unable to understand why the sled wouldn't move as both it and I were still upright. I pulled my sled, tipped it, pushed it, kicked at whatever there might be under it but, no matter what I did – and I was determined to deal with this 'little' challenge by myself – and try as I might to lift the sled over whatever it was, it was hopeless. I couldn't do it. My sled was stuck fast. I looked around to see if I could fathom out what the problem was and then it struck me that it might just be a little tree stump (and yes, it could only be little, no more than ten cm in diameter and about ten cms proud of the snow).

Eventually, Per Thore came trudging back down the trail to where I was. He did not look at all happy but when he tried to push the sled it still would not budge. He went through the same routine that I had just finished. After further investigation he realised that it was a tree stump that was holding the sled firm. He just lifted the sled up and over the stump for me. I got onto the back and Per Thore jumped onto the side, and with both of us on the sled the dogs raced on up the track to join Cathy and the other dogs. It occurred to me that if these eight dogs could pull that load (120 kilo sled + 60 kilo Rona + 80 kilo Per Thore = 260 kilos, if my maths is right) uphill after all they had been through, no wonder I had been having difficulty stopping them!

I wondered whether Per Thore was beginning to regret being the only male on the expedition. There were some things that, even if Cathy and I collaborated, we still could not achieve with the loads we were carrying – although I was still convinced that my sled was probably the heaviest; especially considering the amount of food the dogs ate every day. Per Thore and Cathy's sleds must have been getting lighter and lighter. As we sled back to his dogs, Per Thore admitted that there was no way I would have been able to release the sled by myself. What a relief, at least now I didn't feel such a failure.

It wasn't long before we came to another of those roads in the middle of nowhere and started to sled along the edge when Per Thore unexpectedly took his sled across the road, closely followed by Cathy. Whether any traffic was coming I couldn't tell, as there was no time to look before my dogs careered after them. I was slipping and sliding at an angle, and directly in front of me on the opposite side of the road was a very large waste-bin – and I mean very large. There was no avoiding action I could possibly take: the waste-bin and I were definitely going to collide. I really was not enjoying this at all. But by flinging my body to the left I managed to avoid it by the skin of my teeth as we took a sharp right-hand bend, before accelerating down a hill. It was a fast, crazy trail we were following, a real adrenaline rush. Then as the trail levelled out I realised my next challenge was to sled at high speed past a parked car. The others had avoided it quite easily but I only just managed to skim down the side of it without physically touching it (although I had to quickly move my left hand out of the way) and come to a halt, exhausted and shaking. What a sense of achievement. It appeared we had arrived at our destination. It was quite late in the day and the dogs were really tired after all the challenges that had confronted us. Cathy and I were definitely ready to stop for the day but, try as we might, we couldn't get into the locked cabin and there was no-one around with a key. The whole place was like a ghost town.

Our only option was to keep on going to find a place suitable to stop for the night. When you think you have arrived at your destination after a long, exhausting and difficult day it is really difficult to summon up the energy, and will, to sled on into the unknown, not knowing how long you will have to continue. This is where you have to dig down deep into your reserves to achieve your goal.

It was about six o'clock. Both Cathy and I were still wet from this morning's little interlude with the river and the temperature was dropping dramatically. We hadn't been sledding for long when Per Thore stopped the sleds and asked 'Have you changed your socks?' 'No' we both replied. 'Well, do it now. If you don't with the temperature dropping your feet will freeze into blocks of ice.' We'd kept putting it off but now he made us change immediately. As uncomfortable as it was to expose our wet feet in those freezing temperatures, dry them, put on dry socks and polythene bags (thus keeping a waterproof layer between our socks and the wet boots), we did it willingly and it worked very well indeed. They were much cosier and drier – now we only had to dry our boots when we finally stopped for the night so I, at least, was pleased because my feet had been getting really quite cold. Our naiveté had nearly cost us dear. How stupid could we be? Frostbite is not something you want to add to your accomplishments. Maybe this was another reason why the mushers thought we were too inexperienced? Thank goodness Per Thore was there.

The temperature was dropping and the light was beginning to fade. We set off again along another frozen river to find somewhere to camp near to water. As we appeared to be on water all of the time, I didn't think it could be too difficult. My left shoulder was beginning to hurt; I realised I must have pulled or torn something when I tried to lift the sled off the tree stump earlier on. The trail seemed to go on forever. I wondered how much farther we had to go. I was sledding third that day so my dogs were gradually dropping farther and farther behind. Luckily, the terrain was fairly flat at that time and I didn't need to concentrate too much. Over to my left there was the beginning of a beautiful sunset so I took some photos as it grew more and more spectacular and then suddenly, in a flash, it was gone. A little light relief in what was becoming a particularly difficult and arduous day. We now seemed to be going on forever and the enjoyment of sledding had, at that particular moment, disappeared. I was tired, hungry and in a great deal of pain. I had to dig really deep to enable me to carry on but at least there was one good thing: my feet were now cosy. The dogs were fantastic, pulling such heavy loads. They just continued pitter patter, pitter patter, all day long – they never gave up. Quite an inspiration – they set a very good example. If the degree of difficulty of the trail affected you, you only had to look at the dogs to feel guilty.

Photo 32 – Sunset (see page 123)

However, my concentration was certainly not at its best and I realised that I had lost sight of both Per Thore and Cathy. I was just following the trail they had made when, the light virtually gone, my dogs decided to turn towards the left. Something told me that was wrong so I jumped on the brakes and shouted 'Whoa' at the same time. Well, that seemed to work this time and we stopped – the dogs must have been getting tired. I looked around but couldn't see any sign of sled marks or dog paws except some slightly darker marks in the snow well over to the right. I shouted to my lead dog, Vinga, 'Herra Vinga, Herra' and took my foot off the brake. She had been watching me and now she looked forward and then back at me again 'Herra Vinga Herra' I shouted again (it's a long way to the front of a sled – from the back of a sled to the tip of the lead dog's nose is nearly the length of a coach). She took a step to the right – we would have to cross some more deep, pristine snow with no trail if we were to get back to where I thought Per Thore's track might be – and with some encouragement from me she led the rest of the dogs over to the right and back onto the trail that Per Thore had made and off we went again.

I felt so proud of her and silently congratulated myself that I had gained her trust – we were working well as a team. We raced off down the trail, eventually coming to another place where the trail seemed to disappear. Again the dogs bore left, again I stopped them and shouted 'Herra Vinga Herra'. With just a moment's hesitation, Vinga turned to the right and went back onto what turned out to be the right trail again. Per Thore and Cathy had stopped a little farther along and, although he watched, Per Thore didn't say a word. He just left it to me to direct the dogs.

We sled on for another two hours before finally stopping in front of some cabins. The owner came out and it was obvious he knew Per Thore. This was Soussjav'ri Station, one of the checkpoints for the Finnmark Race that Per Thore had completed just before collecting us from the airport. Apparently, we were going to make this our destination for the night – thank goodness! My shoulder had been gradually becoming more painful ever since we left the area where we were supposed to stop for the night. In fact, by now my arm was by my side and I was in agony. But there were other sledders around and we had to move the sleds so that our dogs were away from theirs; and like it or not, you cannot sled with only one arm – that is, if you don't want the sled to fall over. At that moment it seemed like an impossible task. I certainly knew that I didn't want to do it.

The route we now had to take dictated sledding down a hill, round a sharp left-hand bend, along some flat ground then another sharp left-hand bend to go up a hill to an area where we could unharness the dogs. As we turned left for the first time my sled hit soft snow and I couldn't balance probably due to the searing pain in my shoulder, nor could I hold the sled upright so again it toppled over. The other two had completed their circuit and were about to unharness their dogs when Per Thore realised that I was in trouble. A very tired Cathy came trudging slowly down the hill to help and we got the sled upright; but just as we set off she jumped on to hitch a lift round the next bend and up the hill. Now this expedition was the first time that Cathy had been dog-sledding so, in fact, she was doing very well. However, she had not quite mastered jumping onto the side of a sled for a ride. There was no problem when Per Thore did it but with Cathy – yes, over it went again. 'Oh no' I cried. I was just about exhausted and the thought of lifting the sled again was all too much. However, only Per Thore could lift my sled by himself, so it took both Cathy and I to do it – maybe I should've insisted that the humans ate more.

By the time I had reached our final stopping place, I was nearly in tears with pain. As I struggled to unharness the dogs I realised that I was going to be pretty useless that evening to help with the chores especially feeding the dogs – thank goodness we would not have to pitch the tent. Now part of my ritual, whenever I unharnessed my dogs, would always be to spend a little time talking to them, thanking them for the day's work. In fact, when we were out on the trail I often congratulated them as we sled along if they had worked hard or done something difficult. Today we had worked really well as a team. But now I needed a little space to unharness them, chat to each one and put them on the chains for the night. I didn't think that I would be able to cope with helping with the feeding but I would try. However, right now space, personal space, was essential.

Trying to be helpful, Cathy offered to help me with the dogs. Kind as the thought was, I would really rather have appreciated her carrying the heavy food boxes into the cabin but I was not in the mood for negotiation, argument or chat. My somewhat curt response was 'Thanks but I can manage.' Perhaps she didn't hear me.

Suddenly, all my dogs were unharnessed and secured on the chains and Cathy was gathering her belongings, eager to get into the cabin to dry out the contents of her sled. So I slowly made my way round to each of the dogs to thank them and, in great pain, collected my things and with difficulty made my way through the deep snow into the cabin. My belongings were slipping as I carried them in my arms and trying to stop them was sending an unbearable pain searing through my shoulder. It was obvious to me that I had seriously damaged it, whether it was a torn muscle in the top of my shoulder or ligament damage I had no idea; all I knew was that the pain was excruciating and I couldn't raise my left arm higher than my waist without crying out in agony. The thought that was going through my mind and filling me with dread was that if this was really serious, my expedition would be over. More importantly, it could mean the end of the entire expedition as we needed at least three sleds to carry all the food and equipment!

Having dumped my belongings on my bunk I said to Cathy that I didn't think I could lift the boxes out of my sled and carry them into the cabin – could she help please? I have no idea what the response was as my mind just could not focus; but I knew Per Thore was out there preparing the food for the dogs and both Cathy and I were inside the cabin. Someone had to help him and it didn't look as if Cathy was about to do so. Reluctantly I went back outside to try to do my usual chore. However, I very quickly found out just how much you rely on two good arms to balance properly when negotiating thigh-deep snow as I stumbled far more than usual, crying out in pain as I overbalanced time and time again, putting my right arm down to stop me falling completely. This was just getting stupid so I explained to Per Thore that I was sorry but I was in too much pain and just could not cope; perhaps tonight Cathy could help with the dogs while I would try to cook the meal. I went back inside the cabin and asked Cathy to swap jobs tonight but she didn't look too happy about that idea, especially as I had to ask her to bring the food boxes inside for me as well.

Somehow, we managed to get everything done. Cathy had laid out all her technical equipment on the spare bunk and draped her clothes wherever there was space. Her sleeping bag was hung next to the wood burner in an attempt to dry it out. Luckily the cabin was a very warm one. I was shattered and in a great deal of pain. With the dogs fed and dinner over it was time for some very tired sledders to go to bed. We had travelled 75 kilometres with an average speed of just 9.3 kph since our dip in the river that morning.

As I prepared for bed I started to take off one layer of thermals and, as I raised my right arm, I cried out in pain. Per Thore promised to give me some very good painkillers in the morning but, in the meantime, try as I might, I just could not sleep. I lay on my back trying to relax and ignore the agony; I wanted to let some very-much-wanted sleep wash over me but it was not to be. I just could not get comfortable and every time I moved that searing pain ripped through my shoulder. By now, the other two were out for the count.

As I lay there, it suddenly occurred to me that we had not kept the publicist informed of the crises of the day, so as quietly as I could I got up, found my journal and pen, and crept out into the hallway. Whilst trying to open this trail we would come across cabins which appeared to be in the middle of nowhere. A blanket of snow has a way of tricking you into thinking you are farther away from civilisation than you think. Whereas the two other cabins we had stayed in consisted of just one room, in this one there was an extra room attached and the dry toilet was also situated inside – a luxury. This was probably because it was one of the stops for the Finnmark race. But for now I just wanted somewhere warm to sit and write. We had been using a publicist and updating the website regularly but, in fact, we knew that what everyone was really waiting for (everyone except us that is) was for something to go wrong. It had occurred to me that we had had a day of crises – and have you ever complained that -4°C is too hot? I had words floating around in my head and it seemed sensible to get something down on paper, as I couldn't sleep. In the morning, time would be precious and I thought if I could write the release we could just send it to the publicist for her to deal with back in England. So sitting by another wood-burning fire and with my head-torch on I wrote the following:

Crisis Day on Nordkapp Expedition

As Per Thore, Rona and Cathy set off on Day Four of the Nordkapp Expedition a crisis occurred. As they left camp Cathy's sled failed to land on the snow bridge to the Kautokeino River and landed in the water. Rona went to help Cathy but the ice where she was standing gave way and Rona slipped into the water also. It was up to Per Thore to save the sled. However, all their technical equipment was waterlogged. Their start was delayed as they tried to dry it out putting in jeopardy a live interview with Saga Radio.

To keep them on schedule the trio were due at their next camp site 75k away that night. As the temperature rose to -4°C the warm sunny weather was a godsend to Rona who was wet from the incident but it was not so for the huskies who cannot cope if the temperatures rises above -10°C.

As they were nearing their destination Rona's sled left the trail and got wedged on a tree stump in a snowdrift. In trying to put the 120kg sled back on the trail Rona severely damaged her shoulder making it difficult to guide the sled.

This has put the success of the Nordkapp Expedition in serious jeopardy. The trio finally arrived at the campsite at 9.30 that night leaving little time for rest and recuperation before they had to be up early again to sled another 50k to their refuelling stop.

CHAPTER 6

It Starts to Fall Apart

Somehow, despite the pain, I eventually managed to fall asleep. We were all a little tardy at rising the next morning. I could hardly move my arm and I wondered how I would cope sledding all day. I was really anxious. The idea of doing a 'thought-to-be-impossible trail' really excited me but it was turning out to be very different from what I had imagined. I definitely wanted to achieve the goal but now I was worried in case my torn muscle would ruin everything. Over breakfast I said to Cathy 'I think we have missed a trick here. I think we should have sent a message to Alex about our crisis day. I've written a piece so perhaps we could send it.' However, I was somewhat surprised when she replied 'I'd rather wait until there's a real crisis.' Personally, I was hoping that we had had the worst of it – any more and I might just not make it to the end. So much for my night-time efforts.

I noticed that Cathy kept looking out of the window, watching Per Thore talking to his friends who looked after this cabin. Then suddenly she disappeared outside but I couldn't understand why. Apparently it turned out that she was keen for him to get on with the chores and feeding the dogs. Now, not knowing how we would fare on this expedition, Per Thore had built in some 'slack time', allowing some lee-way in the first part of the trail to see how we performed before we got too far into the wilderness. Maybe it had not occurred to Cathy that because last night's cabin was locked and we had continued along the trail to this one, we were much farther along the trail than we had anticipated being yesterday and, therefore, we had a little extra time in hand. However, we were at the destination he had been aiming for originally – because the dogs had been so tired, Per Thore had hoped to stop earlier. That 'slack time' had been a good idea.

With help, I managed to get most things done. Cathy and I swapped chores: I made the lunch whilst she helped feed the dogs. We prepared the sleds and

Per Thore's friends waved us farewell as we set off on the next leg of our expedition. Per Thore had given me some very strong painkillers but I still tried to ensure that my left arm went no higher than waist level. Luckily for me this coincided with the height of the sled handle – how bad the problem was would only become apparent when I had to manoeuvre the sled.

Our website dispatch had had to wait overnight as the exertions of the day caught up with us, but just before we set off Cathy put the following onto the website:

The going gets tough

Things are getting tougher out here. Rona tore something in her left shoulder yesterday, she came down a hill round a corner (probably too fast) and the sled swung out into a tree stump, and then jammed round the stump in deep snow. The arm is severely compromised and she is running on painkillers this morning. We don't yet know how she will hold out.

First thing yesterday, crossing a snow bridge from our camp on the bank onto the frozen river we were to follow, my sled swung right and broke through the edge of the bridge, with 2/3 of the sled sinking. We finally pulled it out but my still and video camera are ruined. I am still trying to resuscitate the website comms. Everything in the sled was soaked. Rona went into the river with both feet trying to pull it out. And after all that we still had to sled for 70 km to reach our next stop-point.

We are about to leave for another 50 km today, and then tomorrow is a blessed rest day! It won't come a minute too soon.

Amazingly, as we went further north the thaw seemed to have taken a stronger grip. Sledding along the Lesjohka River, which winds its way along a narrow valley between the hills, there were several places where it was collapsing and you could see the water beneath the ice flowing really fast; but the snow and ice on those melting rivers was still incredibly thick. Each layer appeared to be of a completely different hue – snowy white on top, then aqua, then cream and sometimes it even looked green with icicles whilst the water rushed underneath. It was beautiful. In some places we had more snow bridges to cross but our previous experience now made us a lot more careful.

Not long after we had started, we were joined by another team of four sledders each with six dogs – a tourist group doing a circular tour. They passed us whilst we were on a frozen lake. In fact, unbeknown to us, they had been the other group staying at the Soussjav'ri Station, our stop the previous night.

Their sleds were much lighter (just as ours had been on the Charity Challenge) and it was complete chaos at times as their dogs and ours got tangled up as we sled alongside. We had to keep stopping to untangle them before continuing. It brought back those chilling memories of our arrival at Soppero the year before. However, on this expedition these tourists hadn't got the heavy loads that we now had so they could travel faster. We caught up with them as they stopped to mend one of the sleds on the edge of the lake. I was really pleased when we left them behind as we continued on our travels so that there was no repeat of the previous year's chaos. Our path now was taking us across the most amazing white, undulating landscape and as we headed further north we were escaping into areas hardly ever frequented by humans. This was more like it.

To all snowmobile owners and riders I am sorry but I have to confess that I do not like your noisy smelly machines disturbing the silence of such beautiful landscapes (and yes, I have driven a snowmobile myself and even raced one on the Charity Challenge). However, whilst I did not particularly like snowmobiles, occasionally we would come upon some snowmobile tracks and we would be extremely grateful – without them we might still have been out there. The sight of the odd snowmobile track gave us all a little light relief. We were soon to lose these forever on this trail.

I think I may have had a romantic idea of this expedition. I knew it would be arduous because of the concentration and work required to run a sled. But I was looking forward to being in the wilderness and I am used to tolerating tough conditions. However, I was surprised that the weather was overall warmer, in relative terms, in the Arctic than I had expected. The dogs had to work really hard to pull the sleds as well as break trail in the soft snow we were encountering.

This expedition was also not what I had expected in another sense: I thought we would be well away from civilisation, but I suppose that was silly of me. With people receiving phone calls on top of Everest and commercial companies arranging trips to the summit and others phoning from the North and South Pole, there are now very few places left where you can be away from other humans entirely. We can even communicate with those on the Space Station. Extreme sports and holidays are becoming more popular and many feel the desire to live far away from the hustle and bustle of our cities. For our expedition to have taken place entirely in the wilderness, we would have had to have been helicoptered in – hardly an option with 26 huskies. The only way for us to open this trail was to travel through remote but civilised areas on our way to the wilderness.

Breaking trail we may have been but, at times, we seemed to be in the midst of micro-communities all challenging themselves on this icy playground. At one point we came upon three women cross-country skiing. Now while Per

Thore could get his dogs to manoeuvre quite easily, Cathy's and mine always took the shortest route, in other words line of sight. Mine moved slightly to the right to go round the skiers, however, it still made one of them move quickly to the left to avoid being mown down by my sled. But Cathy's dogs just kept on track and the same skier had to take emergency crash avoidance action as Cathy's sled skimmed her poles. Our proposed stop for lunch was crowded with snowmobiles, skiers and loose dogs – it was Friday, start of the weekend, and we were relatively close to civilisation for a change – so we avoided it and drove our sleds over to a more remote area. After the flat rivers and lakes and the congestion we had encountered, I was longing to be away from everyone again and in the wilderness. Well, they always say you should be careful what you wish for. In the distance I could see majestic snow-covered mountains and I just longed to be in their midst. During our lunch break Cathy was using the satellite phone for quite a long time, relaying all the details of everything that had gone wrong that I had put into my unused press release. Well, I suppose it certainly woke up the media interest in us.

The cross-country skiers we had nearly mown down earlier eventually caught up with us. They were intrigued as to what we were doing and started to question us about where we were going. They were fascinated by these wonderful copies of ancient sleds. We were now on the edge of Jeisjavrre, Finnmark's largest lake and to the right were those beautiful mountains I had seen in the distance sparkling in the sunshine whilst we had still been languishing under cloud. As we set off again across the lake, we met some other cross-country skiers and in the distance we could hear the sound of more snowmobiles – a stark contrast to some of the territory we had been in and were just about to encounter again. The lake was twelve kilometres long and eight wide and it seemed to take forever to sled across. For me, I was glad it was flat and easy sledding as it gave a small amount of relief to my injured shoulder.

More importantly, the sun and clouds created a wonderful kaleidoscope of colours on the mountains to the right-hand side of the lake. To the left the terrain seemed to rise slightly and then just disappear. As ever, it was always interesting to turn round on the sled and look back to where we had come from. It always looked so different, giving an added perspective of the land we were in. However, I was really pleased when eventually we began to climb slowly up the mountains at the northern end of the lake. As much as it was a blessing to have flat and easy sledding, after a while it became boring and I think the dogs felt it too. There had been a gradual decrease in speed as our enthusiasm waned and we could see no end in sight. Once we surmounted the rise, there was a slight descent before we climbed again to the summit then a rush down a very long slope. Towards the bottom, there suddenly appeared

Photo 33 — Magic mountains

what looked like a very large hole in the middle of the trail, with Per Thore's dogs going one way whilst mine headed round the other. I felt we just might have another crisis looming. But with some judicial manoeuvring I navigated round the hole and raced up the other side of this open valley.

The mountain to our right was covered with birch scrub and, suddenly, we saw the most intriguing sight, which virtually stopped us in our tracks. Winding its way between these little birch trees was a long train of snowmobiles roaring down round the mountain. All the riders were dressed in the same black leather outfits with black helmets and all the snowmobiles were black. There were so many of them I thought they would never stop coming. It was like watching the 'baddies' from a James Bond film. As we drew into Jotkajavrre and came to a halt there they all were, snowmobile lined up next to snowmobile. About 20 to 30 riders advanced on us with their cameras to take photographs of our dog-sled teams. It was the oddest of sensations to see old and new modes of transport next to each other. We suddenly realised that they were English speaking. Now, we were quite tired of having people around us as we'd crossed the lake so I have to admit that, rather antisocially, Cathy and I flung Norwegian dog commands interspersed with dog names at each other thus saving ourselves from a long explanation of why we were there. (If you were one of those snowmobilers, may I apologise now? It was very ungracious of us and my very poor excuse is that it came at the end of a series of very difficult challenges.)

Whilst we were away on the expedition, at home I received the following email from a Norwegian who had seen our website and had been skiing over the same lake:

> I have just finished a ski journey... We have only just finished travelling over the Finnmark plateau and we found it extremely hard work. We got bogged down big time from the Reisja gorge, and could only travel over the plateau by using the skooter [snowmobile] tracks otherwise we would sink. – Tim

Boy, did I know how he felt. It sounded as though he went through the 'valley of death' as well. It was good to know we were not alone in our struggles.

The Jotkajavrre station is the centre for this area and is where the Finnmark Race starts as it's sheltered by the surrounding mountains. Per Thore moved us off again, but this time just a short distance to take the sleds away from the main trail so that we could put the chains out and unharness the dogs – this was our refuelling stop. It was our chance to rest the dogs and for my shoulder to heal. We had planned to be here for two nights. I was pleased that the trail that day had been mainly along frozen rivers – albeit beginning to thaw, which had made it a little unnerving. As we silently sled along their firm crusts we could hear the rushing, babbling water beneath the ice. There had only been a short section of forest to negotiate and then Finnmark's largest lake which seemed to be never-ending. I can only say it had been the best day possible for an injured arm. With the strong painkillers and by not raising my hand higher than my waist all day or manoeuvring very much (or indeed picking up fallen sleds), I was only getting occasional pains each time the sled jarred. This stop would give us a chance to unload our sleds completely and sort them out.

During this refuelling stop we would stay in a cabin which had three large rooms – a kitchen and two dormitories – and a little hut up a slope a short way from the front door containing a toilet. Not too luxurious: it was of the same design as the one we had come across on the Charity Challenge, with just a plank going from wall to wall over a large hole – but a toilet nevertheless.

We were at the half-way stage and the dogs, Cathy and I were exhausted. Although the dogs would be resting for the next two days, we had a lot of work to do repairing sleds, reorganising them and preparing for the second half of the trail – we would soon be in the unknown for dog-sledding. Where we were was a staging point north of which was uncharted territory as far as our trail was concerned and we would be heading into a far bigger wilderness than we had encountered before. The real challenge was about to begin!

I dumped my sleeping bag and rucksack in the cabin and went to help feed the dogs. This time we collected the water from a fast-flowing stream that ran behind the cabin. Although there was a steep bank to the river it made a pleasant change. Here I could use a bucket – it was so much faster than

Photo 34 – Bedtime writing Photo: C. O'Dowd

Photo 35 – Rest and extra rations for the dogs Photo: C. O'Dowd

ladling the water out of a hole nearly a metre deep and a hundred metres from a camp site – providing, of course, that you did not fall into the river, which was a real possibility.

Per Thore had laid on a treat for us – a sauna. Sheer bliss! An opportunity to get clean and refresh our bodies, it would make a very welcome change from using wet wipes. It's amazing how fast you can do all the chores when a chance to get clean is in the offing. The sauna was hot and relaxing and as I sat on the bench letting the aches and pains flow out of my body, I had a chance to reflect on our journey so far.

My mind wandered back to Soppero the year before where I had had problems with a slack gangline resulting in two injured dogs. We had arrived in Soppero in chaos but eventually order had been restored. We had fed the dogs, dealt with the injuries and, with a storm brewing, the sleds were turned upside down and secured by their ice-anchors behind the sauna. Then there had been a moment for us. I had grabbed my rucksack and followed the others to a large house. Our feet echoed on the bare boards of that spartan building as we were directed to some steep wooden steps leading to the attic floor which was to be our dormitory. Little had we known at the time that it would be for longer than we had anticipated. Inside, there was an enclosed wood-burning fire and twelve mattresses spread around the floor. Brit Marie was going to cook dinner for us for 7 p.m. so we girls had taken advantage of the free time to return to the building sheltering our sleds to have a sauna. It was brilliant: inside there was a pleasant little room with table and chairs and several cans of beer. There had been lots of laughter and chattering as we had undressed and hurried into the sauna. The simple act of washing our hair made us feel great, the sauna was very nearly too hot but very relaxing and we had eventually handed the building over to the guys – but not before we had drunk all the beer.

But here we were at the half-way stage of this 'thought to be impossible' expedition. We desperately needed this stop. We were running out of reindeer meat for the dogs, the technical equipment needed a chance to dry out, my shoulder needed some time to heal and the sleds had taken some severe punishment and we needed to do some work on them if they were to last to journey's end.

Once we had been refreshed by the sauna and by the sheer luxury of putting on clean clothes, we relaxed over our meal. We were just settling down for the evening when the door to the cabin opened and three Norwegian girls and two huskies arrived to share the cabin. We quickly moved our kit into the room Per Thore was using so that they could have a room of their own. In order to let all the technical equipment dry out Cathy had, unfortunately, spread it over one of the bunks – this happened to be my bed so a bit of rearranging ensued.

Our website dispatch tells a tale:

We have reached our halfway point, and are taking a well-deserved rest day, for human and dog alike. Despite our best intentions of an early start, exhaustion from yesterday's dramas left us slow and tired. Even the dogs were unusually subdued as we set out. The morning route was beautiful, following the Lesjohka River, a narrow valley winding through low hills. Fast flowing, there was open water in many places, and several narrow snow bridges to cross. These were done with care, following yesterday's disaster.

For the first time on the trip we met other dog teams, four teams travelling light on a two-day trip. After lunch we crossed Lesjávri, the biggest lake in Finnmark (Norway's northern-most region, which we are currently traversing). The dogs don't like big lake crossings, becoming bored and lethargic without a target to run towards. But the mountains that lay on the distant horizons were beautiful. Next week we will be passing through them.

Now we are curled up in a beautiful forestry cabin, warm and well fed, a fire blazing in the stove. We have had a sauna, and a dip in the partially frozen river. It is time to chill out and enjoy a lie-in in the morning. The only problem remaining is the technical equipment, which was always temperamental but has become far more so since going swimming yesterday. Getting information onto the website is proving difficult. I am about to go and huddle outside in the cold to try and send this report.

On Saturday morning we had an interview scheduled with Sky News. It was meant to be with both of us but, although I was standing next to Cathy's bed, the interviewer asked her a lot of questions and the time ran out before Cathy could pass the phone to me. By then it was time to get up, feed the dogs and have breakfast. It was a foggy start to the day. Per Thore had been up at 6 a.m. when it was -10°C. As we were resting the dogs, instead of the usual quantities that they had consumed so far now we were also giving them extra rations to build them up and improve their stamina for the next part of the trail. The easy part was over, the second half was going to be much farther away from civilisation and a lot harder for both the dogs and we humans. We decided to put the tent up to dry it out then I went to collect buckets and buckets of water from the stream for the dog's breakfast whilst Cathy busied herself sending photographs to the website over the satellite phone and Per Thore did some repairs to the runners of the sleds. We had been over some rocky ground and they had taken a lot of punishment. That day's dispatch to the website was:

Photo 36 — Time for much-needed repairs

Servicing sled runners

A rest day is a chance to service the rest of our kit. Per Thore smoothes off the plastic runners under the sleds with a knife. Our travels do not just take us across soft snow. We have had to cross several roads – an interesting experience as there's no way to brake on tar, and what cars there are travel fast. The tar is not kind to the plastic.

On Tuesday we were travelling over exposed highlands, stripped clear of snow by the howling winds. Rough rock patches scar the runners, as do the large rocks and tree stumps that we sometimes can't avoid bouncing off. Even the icy patches on rivers and the hard-pack snow on snowmobile trails slowly wear the runners down.

Overnight I had not taken any painkillers and now I realised just how bad my arm was – and how strong the painkillers were. I had only been able to lie in one position and by the morning the pain stretched from my neck to my fingers. I've never liked taking medicines and the ones Per Thore had given me had lasted all day! However, I decided to find out how many we had so that I could ration myself to the end of the trail if necessary. We also took this opportunity to relax and get some rest for ourselves as well. I curled up on one of the chairs and wrote my journal, it was pure luxury as opposed to sitting up in a tent leaning on an insecure rucksack with my notebook on my knees and only the light of my head-torch.

Cathy tried to dry the technical equipment and send another dispatch to the website, this time from me:

A word from Rona

I hadn't realised that we would have a rest day but it is a godsend. The trail has been quite arduous, the dogs are tired, there is the equipment to dry out and my shoulder is giving me a lot of pain. I am rationing the painkillers so that they last to the end of the Expedition. The terrain we have travelled through has been incredible – describing it in the book will be difficult. There will need to be lots of pictures. This has been the most fantastic experience especially as I said after last year's trail for Cancer Research UK 'never again'. On Sunday we set off again for the second half which will be even more remote. Watch this space! Rona

That was so true – despite all the difficulties we had with the sleds, soft snow and indeed the terrain itself, the landscape was unbelievably beautiful. But just when everything seemed to be going well, nature would remind us how fragile we were, how small and insignificant compared to its magnificence.

While we were dealing with the media side of things, Per Thore sat on the floor poring over the maps for the coming route. I counted 45 maps littered across the floor. How he knew where to go I don't know but he had got us this far. Now he just had to get us the rest of the way. Cathy then started to write extended captions for the pictures on the website and at one point she looked up, saying 'Keeper of the Chronicles [that's me], what was the name of the river we drove along for most of Wednesday?' 'Kautokeino' I replied and started to spell it for her. Neither of us could quite get our head round Norwegian. Maybe I was going too fast but Cathy thought I was just using every vowel I could think of. I repeated it and once she had tapped it into her computer she eyed me with a look that said 'Am I sure she's not kidding me?'

It suddenly occurred to me that my injury had been reported back to the UK and had been broadcast by Sky News. However, I was unable to contact my family and now I was a little concerned in case they were worried. I hoped they would contact our publicist, Alex, if they were. When one of the yachts had crashed into us on the Round the World Yacht Race I had managed to call them before they heard about it on the News. However, it appeared that the first part of the expedition had finally caught up with all of us and once lunch was finished we all took an afternoon nap.

I washed up after our evening meal while Cathy went off to send some more material to the website and Per Thore and I chatted for some time about last year's trail in Sweden. Then our thoughts turned to Sunday: we were to be off early – but we said that every morning and it didn't always happen. Our aim had been to sled about 50 kilometres each day but everything depended on the weather, the terrain, injuries, how many times the sled went over, the list goes on. Sometimes, everything went well and we could sled a little farther than anticipated but at other times we didn't get so far. The trail we would be trying to negotiate from now on was in a very remote area where usually only skiers ventured. There would be no cabins, so we'd be camping until the end of the trail. There would be no other opportunity to get fresh supplies so we had to ensure that we had everything we needed and that all was in working order.

But now there were 26 dogs to feed, their faeces to clear up and the tent to pack. It was back to walking thigh-high in snow again. I suppose I should have been getting used to it by now, after all it did happen every night when we stopped; but somehow it never got any easier. It was raining when we went out to do the chores, so to pack the tent would have defeated the object. Instead we hung it inside the cabin to dry off again, hopefully before the morning, when we would have to pack it away. We also hoped that the rain wouldn't freeze (wishful thinking on our part); if it did, it would make sledding the next day very difficult as these heavy sleds would just slide over the ice unable to get any purchase. Despite our afternoon siesta, the long hard days of sledding were taking their toll and we were ready for bed.

The cabin was very warm so I had been sleeping only in my underwear; when I went out to the toilet at three in the morning, I put on just a thermal top, my boots and my big thick jacket which was quite long. This staging post had a few buildings on either side with a very large expanse of flat snow (about the size of a football pitch) in the middle. Over on the other side quite a long way away there were a couple of guys, who had been drinking and messing around on snowmobiles. I tried to wait, staying hidden by the toilet, until they had gone before I returned to the cabin; but as I got to our cabin door they were making their way to their own cabin about 100 metres away. I suppose I must have looked as if I had nothing on under the jacket. Anyway, I took off my boots, jacket and thermal and slipped back into my sleeping bag. Not long afterwards the two men came into our cabin and walked into our room. I froze inside my sleeping bag feeling a mixture of very scared and very uncomfortable, gripping the sleeping bag up around my chin. I needn't have worried. The noise they made luckily woke Per Thore and he talked to them in Norwegian. I had no idea what was being said but Per Thore seemed to be persuading them to move on and eventually they left. It was a really unpleasant experience. Thank goodness my knight in shining armour was with us.

Sunday morning brought the snow and a temperature of 0ºC. Cathy put in her dispatch for the website just before we left:

Arctic melt

The one unexpected problem we have encountered is that temperatures are too high. It rained gently for much of last night and this morning feels damp and grey, with temperatures several degrees above freezing. We have yet to use the arctic suits we have with us, wearing merely thermal leggings, Gore-Tex salopettes and heavy jackets (which sounds like a lot but up here is practically beach wear).

High temperatures bring unexpected problems. We carry raw meat (offal) in frozen blocks to feed the dogs. When it is too warm it begins to melt and reek. Ideally the dogs want to run in -10C to -20C. When it is warmer, they overheat and slow down. Hard snow is easier and faster to run on. In softer snow the dogs sink in, and the lead team battles to break a trail. The human can't help by mushing, as there is nothing solid to push against. The sleds, although wood lashed together with twine, and so very flexible, damage more easily in soft snow. Per Thore has already broken a runner.

It is also easier to tip the sleds and jam them. Pulling 120 kgs of sled upright when floundering in thigh-deep snow, with the dogs swimming up to their bellies, is not easy. The rivers and lakes that so often provide us with an easy line through the hills are also beginning to weaken. We find ourselves sledding through pools of slush on the lakes and across narrow snow bridges on the rivers. To our surprise, we are hoping for colder days ahead!

As we set off on the second and more difficult part of the trail, it was overcast and the cloud cover was very low. What a start. We had to retrace our steps back down the mountain towards the lake before turning north and heading off up into the mountains I had seen as we traversed the lake three days earlier. Little did we know that this was just the start of a continual necessity to retrace our steps to find a route to journey's end. It was very different from the first half of the expedition. Everywhere was all white, misty, cloudy and the wind

Photo 37 – We're on our own

made it bitterly cold as we sled along; but in the distance we could see that the cloud was less dense and the sun dappled on the mountains. I was hoping that the mountains now would be more diverse but they all seemed to be the same, rounded with exposed black rocks jutting out in places where the snow was melting. I love mountains normally but these were not looking particularly spectacular. Perhaps that was because I knew it was going to be very difficult sledding up and down them in those weather conditions, or maybe I was just reflecting the overcast outlook.

We went through various wooded areas and climbed even higher before descending to some lakes high in the mountains. It proved to be difficult sledding – the snow was soft and deep which made it really hard going for the dogs as they strained to drag our heavy sleds (now replenished with frozen and dried dog meat) with the snow gradually accumulating underneath, bringing us to a standstill. Precious time was lost as we pulled, pushed, rocked and kicked at the sleds to try to release them from the grip of this silent enemy. Hard snow is much easier on the dogs. The high temperatures and the soft snow make it extremely difficult for the smaller dogs at the front to find a path. As we came down to the tree line again there was another steep hill with a sharp left turn. This time not only was my sled balancing on one runner, it was on the edge of one, but we didn't go over – perhaps that was a good omen for the day.

As we sled across yet another lake we came upon a snowmobile pulling a caravan on skis! Now I thought 'I've seen it all'. Cathy was so astonished that she stopped her sled to take a photograph – and made exactly the same near-fatal mistake I had made the previous year at the beginning of the

Charity Challenge trail. Now it was Cathy's turn. As she took her photograph, she let go of the sled and fell off as the dogs took off. They only stopped once they arrived at the back of the caravan. I think they must have smelt some food around there. She quickly retrieved them and we set off again, this time past some people fishing through boreholes. As soon as we were off the lake we had to start breaking trail again over deep soft snow and we sank up to our knees every time we had to get off the sled. It made the runners very icy so our feet kept slipping off. The dogs were finding it especially hard to pull the sleds on this uncharted ground and we were really having to search to find a way through.

In the middle of this wild expanse of whiteness, we started to cross yet another lake. The temperature was fluctuating so much that the surface of the lake had melted and refrozen, making it a beautiful aqua colour but somewhat mushy. I have to say, this surface definitely came under the heading of 'suspect'. The sleds were slipping and sliding over the wet surface and the dogs' feet skittered about as they tried to find some purchase. Once on the other side, we continued round the edge of the lake but this involved having to negotiate our way over rocks. Unfortunately, my dogs decided they were going to take control and go a different way to everybody else, across another very slushy

Photo 38 — Melting lakes Photo: C. O'Dowd

green lake. To say the least, I found this most disconcerting as I wondered just how much it had thawed and whether it might give way under the weight of our heavy load.

Cathy's dispatch that day read:

Sleds afloat

The surface ice on the lakes is beginning to melt, leaving the ice a strange pale green colour. The dogs are running through an inch of water.

Eventually to our right we could see another range of really lovely mountains. We had been heading north all day when suddenly we came to a halt. At first I wondered why but as Per Thore started to put out the chains for the dogs, I realised that this was to be our campsite. I had been concentrating on taking in the surroundings as well as trying to keep the sled moving so had lost track of time. It had been a difficult day's sledding and it was not going to get any easier now. Per Thore tried drilling for water but the lake was frozen to the bottom. We would have to melt a lot of snow to provide water for the dogs and ourselves. It was bitterly cold as we unharnessed the dogs and, using the sleds as windbreaks to protect them, we put up the tents. I dug all the snow onto the flaps and started to unload our personal belongings from the sled but, unfortunately, Cathy had not finished digging out the snow hole inside the tent for the kitchen. She made the comment 'Some of us do all the work whilst others stand around with bits of kit'. I think that may well have been directed at me – there certainly wasn't anyone else around. I retorted that as she had had her belongings in a black plastic sack having only just got them all dried; if I got them wet again my name would be mud. Tensions were definitely rising. However, these were really the only times when we sniped at each other, when we had finished a hard day's sledding, we were tired and there was still lots of work to do. Luckily it never amounted to anything nor lasted very long. I think at most the odd comment was fired as a warning shot over the bows. We didn't really know each other very well before we embarked on this expedition and it would have been surprising if there had been no friction at all, particularly in these conditions.

It really was bitterly cold and as soon as we had eaten a big pasta meal we all went to bed, snuggling deep into our sleeping bags – it was only 7.30 p.m. but we were to be up by 6 a.m. the following day, when the colder temperature would be better for the dogs. Yet again they had worked extremely hard all day.

Cathy's website dispatch read:

Soft and slow

We have covered just 50 km, but we are pleased to have come even that far. Conditions today turned out to be as bad as we feared. It has been a slow-going day, floundering through soft, deep snow for hour after hour. It is equally frustrating for the lead team, which has the hard job of trail-breaking, and for the teams that follow, which are continually braking. As the brakes don't work well in deep snow, quickly clogging and jamming, it becomes a process of continually stopping and starting again.

The dogs hate working in these conditions and we need to get them onto firmer ground. If the weather stays like this we need to travel much earlier in the day when the snow is still hard. Currently the plan is dog feeding at 4 a.m., leaving at 6 a.m. We just can't wait!

The next morning we set off at 6.45, which was good for us – it was light, crisp and chilly. At first the mountains had that now-familiar rounded shape with black rocks protruding where the wind had whipped away the snow – not very exciting but the snow was crisp and so easier for the dogs. Per Thore made for a river, the melting river I called it, but its real name was Bastinjåkka. Dog-sledding along frozen rivers is technically simple – unless, of course, they are melting. This particular river was definitely thawing and there were big holes in the ice with clear bubbling water visible. Having nearly fallen into a melting river the previous year, these were now, as far as I was concerned, a source of high adrenalin impact – or fear! However, this one seemed OK. Well, I thought it was. It looked beautiful, but you have to remember that Per Thore's dogs did as he told them while the dogs coming behind liked to see where his dogs were going and take a shortcut.

Cathy's dispatch was:

River riding

After slow and rough progress over the highlands, we picked up speed as we followed the Bastinjåkka river. It provided a fast and level highway north for several hours, paved in pale-green ice, although with some alarming cracks and holes. Finally it veered away from north, and we headed back into the hills, heading in all innocence into the valley of death.

We were swinging crazily from one side of the river to the other to avoid the open water when suddenly we started going up the right-hand bank and turned a corner. I was second in line that day but we still had quite a distance between us when Per Thore pointed down and shouted something to me – I couldn't hear him – his words were whipped away on the wind. As my dogs raced after him I looked in the direction he was pointing just as my sled slid past the very spot. I flung myself wildly to the right to avoid a mound of snow with a very large hole beneath it – a very large expanse of nothing for us to drop into. Cathy was some way behind but I turned and pointed out the hole to her hoping she would be able to avoid it. I just managed to indicate it to her as she arrived at the crucial spot.

Part of the time we had been sledding through surface water, sliding all over the place, but we had just got onto terra firma again when my gangline broke. Luckily, Per Thore was not very far ahead and my lead dogs stopped next to him, so all I had to do was just move the other dogs close up to him so that he could mend it. Off we went again. This was more like it – much more exciting. We were breaking new ground so we were constantly twisting and turning trying to find the right way to go. Now we were really exploring – this was what I had come for. The scenery was so stunning with scrubby trees dappling the side of the brilliant snow-covered mountains and we were the only ones there. It was phenomenal! It had been -20°C overnight and every day my eyes just streamed because of the cold air. I didn't like wearing goggles as they stopped the air getting to my eyes but my sunglasses were also nearly all-encompassing, though with small air vents. I just had to tolerate my eyes streaming, but it was the lesser of two evils. The weather was bitterly cold and the wind was biting – biting through my sunglasses and biting at my cheeks.

This wild open landscape reminded me of the Southern Ocean where the scenery was continually changing and always filled me with awe. You expect it to be all the same but it is only when you experience it that you realise just how diverse it is. The light, colours and hues are forever reworking the landscape. We were in the Norwegian Arctic, alone on top of the mountains. It was a wilderness of incredible beauty. We would sled over snow, rocky outcrops laid bare by the vicious winds, across moss as it clung to the rocks, over giant tufts of grass which made the sled tumble from side to side, over melting lakes or deep snow clawing at the sled to drag it to a standstill. Then suddenly it would be hard underfoot and all the time the dogs kept running as fast as the terrain, the sleds and the two inexperienced humans would allow. They coped so well. The only sound was the swoosh of the sleds across the iced snow. I couldn't get over how beautiful it was with the deep blue sky, unbelievably cold, but no longer as overcast as the previous few days. Every which way I looked as we climbed higher and higher we were surrounded by mountains and as we descended the wind would sting any exposed flesh. We were doing over 20 kph – it was imperative now to brake so that the heavy sleds wouldn't outrun the dogs and harm them. By now I was in third place and the two sleds in front streamed down the mountains, so tiny bits of snow and ice rose like ostrich feathers from their brakes, often being thrown straight into my face.

These fluctuating spring temperatures were producing nightly a crispy layer of ice over the snow which tore at the soft skin of the dogs' paws resulting in us having to put bootees on some of the injured paws to protect them. But this raised yet another new problem. The force required to pull the sleds ripped the bootees off their paws. Whoever was sledding behind had to swerve to pick up the offending bootee so that it could be reunited with its owner. The dogs would also take every opportunity when we stopped to inch their paw closer and closer to their mouth so they could surreptitiously use their teeth to tease the Velcro apart (how's that for evolution?) and lose the bootee that was detracting from their macho image. This bootee also had to be reunited with the correct paw, much to the chagrin of its owner.

When the snow was impassable we had to turn round, retrace our steps and try to find a different route. Beneath the thin layer of ice the snow was so soft and sticky that it was a challenge to push the sleds. Breaking trail was tough, and if things went wrong the next sled tended to get caught in the same rut. Not only that, whenever you went back to help the other person you would sink up to your thighs in snow, making it really difficult to get back to your own sled. You could feel your strength being slowly sapped away. Our progress was slow as we pushed the sleds up the mountain towards the pass, because they continually toppled. We turned this way and that but it was almost impossible to make any real progress. It was becoming a nightmare. I think Per Thore felt we were trying to sabotage his efforts as he suddenly turned his dogs round towards a valley whose correct name was Gukkesgurro, but before the day was out Cathy and I were to rename it the Valley of Death. Our nightmare did not stop. We had changed course and come this way because it was meant to be easier but this valley was not much better than the pass. Time and time again we had to pick up the sleds as we tried to negotiate the trail Per Thore made for us. Over went my sled again, and I was still trying to untangle myself when Cathy, now out of control, crashed into me, pinning my leg between the two sleds. Luckily, although it was dangling over the raised runner, my leg didn't break. Cathy's dispatch for the website read:

> After our breakfast break we innocently sled straight into the valley of death. Deep snow got deeper, soft snow got softer, and we began to climb the valley side in search of harder, shallower snow. That proved a fatal mistake. Traversing steep slopes in deep snow was asking for the sleds to tip over time and again. And when they went, they tipped well past the horizontal, leaving us pushing desperately upwards while mired in thigh-deep snow. Here, Per Thore rescues Rona's sled.

Photo 39 — More than 90 degrees

Securing her sled, Cathy got off and came back to help me. However, this time the sled was over more than 90° so we needed Per Thore's help. Once all was restored to normality, Cathy went off only to narrowly miss a scrubby birch tree. Seeing that, I made a mental note to steer my dogs away from it. They say that whatever you put in your mind you get. Well, maybe it was because I was mentally saying to myself 'keep clear of the tree' as we set off that my dogs went to the left and the sled veered to the right with the result they were on different sides of the tree. Have you ever tried pulling eight dogs backward when they want to go forward? My heart sank. How on earth was I to pull a sled weighing 120k plus eight strong dogs backwards up a hill on slippery snow that I could get no purchase on? Cathy stopped her sled and plodded back to where I was whilst Per Thore looked on. Yet again I wondered whether he was regretting taking us on the trail, especially that day. Poor Cathy was on the back of my sled ready to pull it free from the tree and I was between the sled and the dogs holding onto the gangline, trying to pull my dogs backwards. We only needed six inches to escape from the tree. But it was no good, the feat was totally impossible for us.

Eventually, Per Thore turned his dogs round and came back up the hill. Now with me on the back of the sled, Per Thore holding my dogs and with both of us pulling them backwards, the tree gave up its hold on us and we were released. Off we went again zig-zagging round trees – it was definitely a case of teamwork here. Twisting and turning down the sides of the valley which were thick with snow, relief hit me as we came to an open space. But why had my sled stopped? Once again the sticky soft snow had built up so much under the sled that it had brought me to a standstill. I was trapped. The sledding was tremendous but the spring thaw made the conditions extremely difficult and took their toll on us both physically and mentally. As we were exploring and this was totally new terrain, we had no idea when these conditions might change or end. Per Thore and Cathy had disappeared through a gap, down the hill and round the corner but I was going nowhere. I pushed, I pulled, I kicked, I waggled the sled backwards and forwards in an effort to get it to move but I didn't dare tip it to the side for fear it would go over and I would be stuck with no advance or rear guard in sight.

Suddenly I was off again following the trail the others had made – boy, was it a steep slope! There was the inevitable sharp left-hand bend at the bottom and – no, you're wrong – I negotiated it feeling very proud of myself as I had also managed to pick up a bootee on the way. But, pride comes before a fall they say and predictably just past the bend, the snow was soft and my sled toppled in and so did I. However, this time I managed to get it up again on

Photo 40 – Rona traversing downhill Photo: C. O'Dowd

my own. Off I went but my balance was all wrong and over I went again. This time comprehensively – this was now getting tedious.

One of the hardest parts of the expedition was having repeatedly to lift these heavy sleds and get them through the thawing snow. I was exhausted. It was at those times that self-doubt would creep in and I would start wondering whether I was too old to do this. The going was certainly tough now, we were trying to do 70 kilometres, and we had made slow progress and should already have arrived at our destination, having started so early. But our speed was determined, as always, by the dogs and the conditions we had to negotiate.

Cathy's dispatch for the website was:

Rona ramps valley of death

Having given up on our attempt to traverse out of the valley of death, we did a kamikaze run straight down to the valley floor. Here Rona charges down the final incline. We had our feet so hard on the foot brake that our feet were nearly half a foot below the sled runners and still we ploughed down through the soft snow. We finally exited the valley via a pass at its head and found hard-packed snowmobile trails that carried us speedily northwards.

Cathy's description of my downhill sledding at this moment was:

Rona demonstrates the art of traversing a slope with a heavy sled. Both feet on the uphill sled runner, and weight is pushed as far up the hill as possible, butt swinging wide, to try and stop the sled sliding downhill.

Just when I thought I'd got the hang of dog-sledding, had got the balance right and was not falling off, I went into numerous falls. I was hot, sticky, smelly, sweating, exhausted, fed up, tired of cold stingy winds and tired of white mountains. This was no glamorous life – if only you could have seen me then. It was blood, sweat and tears.

Once back on top of the mountains we had to stop yet again in a very exposed spot as I tried to help Cathy with her sled; but then, despite having put the ice anchor in, my sled started to move. I obviously hadn't put it in far enough. I grabbed the anchor and was pulled along the trail in a prone position. Cathy managed to jump onto my sled and stop it. Per Thore's face said 'Oh no, Rona's off again.' I picked myself up and got back on to my sled, that is, the one Cathy was on and she went back to her sled and with order restored we moved off again. By now I think Per Thore was so confused by the two of us that he just started moving on. At last we negotiated the slope where I had kept falling over. As we came down the mountain the trail was harder snow, packed and bumpy, which made it a little easier for the dogs to run but difficult for us to keep them under control. Per Thore and Cathy were well ahead and Vinga started to go to the right. I stopped the sled and shouted 'Vance Vinga'. She looked at me and then obeyed. Once again I was feeling really quite pleased that my dogs were trusting me.

I took a drink to refresh myself a bit – the sun was trying to come through the clouds and the scenery was fantastic again. It's moments like that that make the expedition worthwhile – moments to be savoured and stored for when the times get hard again as they surely will.

Not only did we have this unknown terrain to deal with but there were still publicity calls to make during this eventful morning. As Cathy put on the website:

> During our break, Rona entertained the Oxford commuter traffic
> on BBC Radio Oxford.

Oxford seemed a million miles away. Everywhere we looked the scenery was just white and black, but the wind was still bitingly cold. Cocooned from head to toe in thermals and Gore-Tex, you are lulled into a false sense of security about the intenseness of this cold. Inside your man-made shell your body heat increases in line with the exertion being expelled. But hesitate: if you think it prudent to peel a layer, the true story will be revealed as the icy blast whistles round and stings any exposed skin. At this moment, I was all too well aware that now was not a good moment to remove anything.

We sled down through a little forest turning this way and that whilst Per Thore looked for a frozen river so that we could cross one of those rare isolated roads. The trail was quite good and we were travelling at 15 kph. In fact, try as we might we could not find our way onto the river so in the end we had to cross it by a road bridge, which brought a new challenge. We sled along the verge until we came to the bridge – then came the tricky bit. We had to move out onto the road to negotiate the bridge. One by one we went up the slope onto the road: first Per Thore, then Cathy and finally me, a little way behind. Once over the bridge Per Thore turned to the right to get back onto the verge, followed by Cathy. I was in the centre of the bridge when round the corner at the top of the next hill came a very large lorry heading straight towards me. There was nothing I could do, I couldn't brake I was on the road and there was nowhere to go anyway. The other two had stopped to see what would happen. I just had to keep going and at the same spot where Per Thore turned onto the verge I called to Vinga to go right which luckily she did without hesitation. Phew! I waved a thank you to the lorry driver who had kindly slowed down for me.

Once I was on the verge, the others moved off and we went up the hill to a road junction, in fact it was a T-Junction – well this was certainly a first.

Another crossing to negotiate and this time we had traffic coming from three directions. It took a lot of patience to be able to find a large-enough gap in the traffic so that each sled could get across the junction safely. Once we were over the road junction, the next obstacle awaited: we had to drive the dogs up a very steep bank on the other side of the road which took us to into a forest with yet more trees to negotiate before we came to the edge of a lake. Here we suddenly came to a halt. Apparently, this was where we were to make our camp for the night.

Photo 41 – It was a tough day! (see page 124)

With the dogs unharnessed and on the chains, Per Thore took his two-metre ice drill to the middle of the lake to bore the usual two holes. Whilst Cathy started to erect our tent I slipped and slid towards the holes with my ladle and rigid insulated bag. Meanwhile, Per Thore returned to the campsite and started chopping the frozen reindeer meat. The routine was the same every time we stopped. However, this time, while we were eating Per Thore quietly asked if we had counted the number of times our sleds had gone over. Laughing, my reply was 'No, I can't count that high!' I was so pleased there were three of us. It made the atmosphere less intense and I was certainly glad Per Thore was leading the team. Apart from the fact that he is a good friend, he is very easy going and comfortable to get along with. He's the sort of guy I felt I could talk to about anything.

Whilst he helped me to feed the dogs one day he had explained that his friends, who were very experienced mushers, thought that this expedition would not work. We were going places only skiers went – not dog-sleds. They thought the sleds were too heavy and that Cathy and I were too inexperienced. They thought that he should not start the expedition from Signaldalen as, with such heavy sleds, we would never get up the first mountain through the forest, let alone to the Three Nations Border. They thought the sleds would break as we tried to get up to the border. Usually dog-sled trips were done in a circle, if the mushers were not very experienced, so this was something completely different. But Per Thore wanted to open up the trail for dog-sleds and he believed that we could do it. Per Thore was very patient, he would just let us get on with it and only helped if it was something we could not manage. He never got angry unless the dogs were put in danger.

It looked as though there would not be much sledding still to do – maybe one more day on the mainland and then one more to sled the final island to get to Nordkapp. We were due to meet Ryno at Kåjford, the end of the mainland. He was going to drive the dog-trailer up to meet us at that point and then drive us through the tunnels under the sea connecting the islands. We would drive across the islands to the island of Mageröya on which stands Nordkapp. In the tent that night I wrote in my journal 'So tomorrow we should see the sea. I am glad that I have done this trail – whether I ever dog-sled again I don't know.' However, on a more down-to-earth note, right now we were still trying to dry the insoles to our boots – still wet from our little escapade on the Kautokeino River.

Photo 42 – Drying the insoles (see page 124)

As we sat in the tent talking, the dogs performed their twice daily ritual, howling their thank you for their meal. It must have been 40 minutes since we had fed them. As they do it every time we feed them we decided that we ought to make a sound recording for the website. I suggested using my little Dictaphone – this had proven to be a really useful tool to record comments on how I was feeling and what the scenery was like when we were sledding. However, Cathy decided that the recording sounded like banshees and not huskies so decided to record the howling straight onto the satellite phone. Whilst we discussed the best way to do this we took our eye off the ball and the inner soles of my boots received a bit of a scorching from the Primus! It was getting quite late but my feet were only just beginning to get warm. Eventually we slid into our sleeping bags and allowed sleep to wash over us; but I did have time to write in my journal: 'As I lie on the cold snow in this cold tent I am thinking of my big bed at home with its cosy enveloping big duvet.' But for now we still had a long way to go…

Photo 1 — Training in Andorra

Photo 3 — Finishing the sleds

Photo 4 — Per Thore and the maps

Photo 6 — The rest of the team

Photo 7 — Hege and Jomar returning from a training run

Photo 12 — Navigating the tarmac highway Photo: C. O'Dowd

Photo 13 — The life-saving drill Photo: C. O'Dowd

Photo 15 — The offending fence Photo: C. O'Dowd

118

Photo 17 — Ice-blue melting lakes Photo: C. O'Dowd

Photo 19 — Leaving Reisa National Park Photo: C. O'Dowd

Photo 22 — Lunch by the reindeer fence Photo: C. O'Dowd

Photo 26 — Rona testing the water Photo: unattributed

Photo 27 — Cutting wood to cook the dinner

Photo 28 — Too hot to sled

Photo 29 — The latest in doggie footwear

Photo 31 – Rona's downhill

Photo 32 – Sunset

Photo 41 — It was a tough day!

Photo 42 — Drying the insoles Photo: C. O'Dowd

Photo 45 – Cooling down Photo: C. O'Dowd

Photo 44 – A blood-stained Rona Photo: C. O'Dowd

Photo 50 – Do we have to sled? Photo: C. O'Dowd

Photo 51 — Naughty Sally! Photo: C. O'Dowd

Photo 53 — We made it!

Photo 54 — I did it! Photo: C. O'Dowd

Photo 55 — Sally and Vinga — we're off

Photo 57 — Cooking en route

Photo 58 — The turf house

Photo **60** – Per Nils in Sámi clothes

CHAPTER 7

To the Top of Europe

That night was incredibly cold. I could get neither comfortable nor warm, and it was made worse because I needed to go outside twice – usually it was only once. The wind was bitter as I left the tent but seeing the sun on the distant mountains soon reminded me why I was there. It was like being in a black-and-white film and I would become ecstatic whenever we were sledding if I saw a bird or a tree – anything that had just a little bit of colour.

That day we were due to sled 80 kilometres in order to meet up with Ryno.

Photo 43 – Frozen trail Photo: C. O'Dowd

The ground was frozen and overnight our waterhole had closed over so Per Thore had to come down with me to break the ice with a very large sharp knife he keeps on his belt. Once breakfast was over and we had packed the sleds, we set off across the lake before joining another melting river. As we gradually worked our way back up into the mountains, the snow was cold and crisp. The mountains as ever were beautiful and I enjoyed my game of looking back to see where we had come from. As we went higher the temperature gradually got colder until the wind chill was -15°C. It went straight through me and at one point, when Per Thore paused, I grabbed the opportunity to put my neck warmer on in order, hopefully, to stop the wind stinging my cheeks. We had a see-saw ride up the side of one mountain, round the corner and then down the other side before going up and then down them again. The views of the mountains were continually changing. As we came around some corners, there in front of us we would see these aqua blue lakes which had started to thaw and then frozen solid again, which giving them this very pretty colour.

Photo 44 – A blood-stained Rona (see page 126)

We came down the side of a steep, snow-covered mountain and my dogs saw that Per Thore's dogs were going round a corner to the left, so they decided to take a shortcut. By now I had a strong suspicion that my sled had a magnet on it. The problem was that, just to the left of our trail, a rock was jutting out from the snow. I hung out to the right to move the sled round it. Not a chance. The next thing I knew 'BANG' the sled hit the rock and fell over on its side as I did a magnificent swallow-dive, flying several feet head first into the hard packed snow where I lay for a moment somewhat stunned. The sled slid on its side for a few feet planting the ice anchor firmly in the snow. I was dazed and took a moment or two to recover. Cathy, who had been sledding behind me, now ran up to see if I was l alright. Per Thore had also come to see if I was OK. I could hear Per Thore ask Cathy 'Do you think she is alright?' I didn't hear her response as I was wondering if my sunglasses had broken and whether there was any glass in my eyes. Slowly I started to get up, the bridge of my nose hurt and my head ached. Per Thore and Cathy picked up my sled, then they helped me up and reunited me with it. Just as they were returning to their own sleds Cathy took another look at me and said 'Hold on a moment.' Lifting my sunglasses she revealed lots of red blood pouring down my face. Out came the First Aid kit and she cleaned the wound up – but not before she had taken a photo of me. You always know who your friends are when you do something like this: they're the ones taking a photo of you looking somewhat less than your best, then they put it on a website for the world to see.

As Cathy said, 'Rona, there was 10,000 square feet of snow and one rock – and you hit it!' I now have a nice scar on the bridge of my nose. The website dispatch for this close encounter was:

First blood spilt. The first expedition blood to be spilt is Rona's. The team was sledding down a slope, moving fast on hard snow. In the middle was one rock, which Rona unerringly hit. She was thrown from the sled, face-planting in the snow, cutting herself on the bridge of her nose. She picked herself up, got back on her sled and we continued – no other choice really!

We set off once more, but I was a little nervous as we wove our way in and out of clumps of rock and then went haring down the sides of mountains, turning corners at the very last moment. It did not help that Cathy's dogs would run alongside mine making manoeuvring even more difficult. As we made our way zig-zagging down the mountain, Per Thore turned his sled towards a stretch of open water and I thought for a moment that he expected me to sled over it! To my relief he was only stopping to fill his flask with the clear, ice-cold mountain water. Each time we did stop the dogs took the opportunity to roll in the snow and try to eat it.

Photo 45 – Cooling down (see page 125)

Per Thore started going up another mountain, stopped and turned his dogs back. Whether it was his instinct and knowledge of the Arctic Circle or whether it was a sound he heard or a smell, I do not know; but he turned to the right in order to go over a lower part, telling us as we did that we had to hold onto the sleds no matter what. I couldn't see any reindeer, the usual reason for these instructions; but as we turned the corner there was a whole herd of them spread out on various snow-free tufts of moss. Unfortunately, we had inadvertently frightened them which made them run – not away from us but in the same direction. As we sled along, my dogs suddenly realised that these animals racing alongside were reindeer and turned towards them. I think they thought 'Oh good, supper on the hoof!' I had to keep shouting 'Vance Vance' to get them back on track. It was an amazing sight to see a herd of reindeer in the wild running alongside us. However, the last thing we wanted was for the reindeer to drop their calves early because our dogs had frightened them. To take photographs whilst trying to steer our sleds as they were careering along was extremely difficult but this was a must. Then some of the reindeer decided to be very obliging by running beside my sled across the snow. As we sled further down towards sea-level we left the reindeer high on the mountains, negotiated another road, went up a steep bank and on uphill to another range of mountains. If we looked to the right, we could see glimpses of the sea, losing sight of it again as we tried to sled over a frozen lake.

Per Thore was doing all the navigating with GPS, compass and maps as we broke new ground. It was amazing how all the mountains now looked the same to me, snowy white with those protruding black rocks – somehow I had

Photo 46 – Reindeer Photo: C. O'Dowd

anticipated a much greater variation in shape. And how Per Thore read the map when everywhere looked so much the same was beyond me. We spent some considerable time roaming over the mountain tops, turning one way and then retracing our steps and turning another, trying to find a way through. We were continually thwarted either by an overhang or open water – it was becoming very frustrating. So maybe he too was having some difficulty. But exploring all possibilities is what you have to do if you are trying to break a trail.

Eventually we found a possible route which turned out to be the most hair-raising switchback ride. We raced over jagged rocks, twisting and turning to find a route down the mountainside. As we got lower, where the snow had melted, there were large tussocks of grass standing proud of the ground which threw the sled from side to side. It had been scary enough on the rocks but I thought the grassy tussocks were even worse. I was terrified as we hurtled down that last mountain to Kåjford and finally came to a halt at sea level. What a relief! I had just about had enough and I think if someone had said the wrong thing at that moment, I would have snapped. I was finding it really hard to hold myself together. I think the nosedive followed by that horrendous race down the mountain with hardly any snow was the final straw. We had one more day to sled and I really didn't know whether I would be able to cope.

The website update read:

Rock dodgems

As we approached the coast (which is warmed by the Gulf stream) there was less and less snow, making for interesting navigation through the rocks and grass hummocks.

But for now, the relentless work continued. We set up camp that night next to the sea; we were at the end of the mainland. It was still very cold so again we sheltered the tents with the sleds. Unfortunately, the only place to harness the dogs was in swampland. Boy, did I feel for them. We had sled 80 kilometres over very difficult terrain with an average speed of 10.2 kph (though our fastest speed had been an extraordinary 26.5 kph) and they had had to contend with mountains, rocks and grassy tussocks, only to be rewarded by a night sleeping in a cold swamp. I could empathise with each one of them and gave mine an extra stroke and apologised to them. They certainly deserved better; they were simply amazing animals and I could understand Per Thore's attachment to them. I think Per Thore must have realised how I was feeling – or else he was just frustrated that I was taking so long to get on with the work – as he started to collect water from a very fast flowing river just before

Photo 47 – Switchback ride Photo: C. O'Dowd

it went under the road and escaped to the sea. As I started to collect more water, he warned me to be careful that I didn't fall in, but walking back to the campsite over those deceptive tussocks was difficult. You would think you were on firm ground and then realise that beneath the grass was a deep dip. So whilst I didn't actually fall into the river, I did spill a fair amount of the water I was carrying down me.

As we neared the end of the trail we were coming to the end of the dispatches being posted on the website. The one Cathy posted for that, hopefully, penultimate day of the expedition read:

> We have done a total of 515 kilometres. After our soft-snow nightmares of the past few days our prayers were answered in bone-chilling fashion. Clear skies and sunshine made for beautiful vistas, but low temperatures and fierce winds made it probably our coldest day yet. Hard crisp snow made for very rapid progress. However, dogs and humans are deeply tired and many of the dogs have bleeding paws. The day's high was sledding through herds of reindeer, the low Rona swan-diving off her sled to face-plant in the snow. Late in the afternoon we descended from the highlands to see the sea deep blue ahead of us and the mountains of Nordkapp in the distance. Tomorrow we will stand on Europe's northern-most point. While it is exciting to see our goal so close, it is also sad to see the experience drawing to a close.

We had our meal and there was hardly any conversation before Per Thore went off to his tent and we got ready to sleep. Was that because we were all tired or because we knew we were coming to the end of this extraordinary expedition and would soon be going our separate ways?

We were just settling down to sleep when Per Thore called to us. At long last there were some Northern Lights. It took me back to the previous year when we had been in Soppero and the storm had finally passed. Our return journey was to start the next day, no matter what the weather was like and so, as soon as supper was over, we had said our goodbyes to Brit Marie and Per Nils. It was then time to sort out our rucksacks, bring the frozen harnesses in to thaw and turn the sleds upside down to clear them of snow. We had just been settling down for the night when the cry had gone up 'Northern Lights!' Struggling into boots and jackets and little else we had raced downstairs to be rewarded by the most astonishing display as intense swirls of green pulsed and vibrated across the heavens above. We had stood there transfixed, watching the sky in amazement – not a word had been spoken, just 'Oooos' and 'Ahhhhhs' as the heavens danced in front of our eyes. Despite having no Arctic suits on we had been so mesmerised by this incredible spectacle that seemed to cover

Photo 48 – Last camp of the trail? Photo: C. O'Dowd

the entire sky, no-one had felt the cold as we had watched. Every so often we could see just a hint of purple appearing along the edge. It had been the first time I had ever seen the Northern Lights and they were fantastic, certainly living up to their reputation. They remained for ages, pulsing and changing shape and colour. Eventually they had begun to fade and as they did so the cold had made itself felt in no uncertain terms. One by one we had returned to the warmth of our beds, by which time the temperature outside had risen to -15°C.

However, Cathy had never seen them before. As we scrambled out of the tent, it was hard to differentiate between the Northern Lights and a wispy cloud, but they were just about discernible, although it was a very light shower indeed. Nothing like the incredible display Per Thore and I had seen at Soppero the year before. Per Thore tried to convince us that they would get better, but eventually we gave up and scurried back to the warmth of our tent. We had just settled down when Ryno arrived at our campsite, having started his long drive north in the early morning. We started to put on our outer gear when Per Thore told us to get some rest: he and Ryno would put the dogs into the trailer with clean dry straw. After a catch up chat and coffee, we thought that Ryno would share Per Thore's tent but, instead, he slung his hammock between the truck and the trailer, slipped into his sleeping bag and 'hit the hay'. As Cathy and I settled down to sleep after a long and arduous day I realised that my left thigh and right hip were badly bruised. Whenever I turned over in my sleeping bag I squealed in pain – I made a mental note to avoid isolated rocks on snowy mountains in the future. That is, if there was a future. The snow we were lying on was really hard – it was the ultimate orthopaedic bed.

Next day when I woke up my feet were cold, my back ached, the base of my thumbs were painful and the ends of my fingers hurt – but not badly, considering what we had been through. I rubbed my hands over my face and nearly knocked off the newly formed scab on my nose from yesterday's fall. So this is my glamorous life? I think people who think this should have seen me on this expedition – however, I suppose a lot did once Cathy had put that lovely picture of me on the website! I had had only one sauna in ten days, I couldn't sleep properly either due to injury, cold or the bumpy terrain and, the mirror that Cathy had brought with her revealed that my eyes looked tired and puffy. So much for glamour.

When we had arrived at this campsite the night before, the sun was shining on the mountains that encircled the bay and it had looked beautiful; but now the mountains were beneath a big cloud, which rather reflected my mood. I definitely needed a coffee. Ryno and Per Thore took all the dogs out of the trailer to feed them whilst Cathy and I got on with making breakfast and lunch. Usually, Per Thore would appear as soon as the coffee was made but, strangely, he did not seem to smell it this morning. Was he tired of searching for a route for us to follow? What had caused the change in him? Maybe knowing the amount of effort that Ryno had to put in to reach us, he wanted to finish feeding the dogs first. We were hoping that this would be our last day on the

Photo 49 – Nearly there

trail and I was aching like mad. That night, hopefully, we would have finished the trail and would be able to spend the night in a hotel. Was I looking forward to a hotel bed? You bet I was! But more to the point, I would be able to have a shower – now that can only be called a little piece of heaven on earth.

Could we take things a little easier now? Definitely not. Cathy and I had decided that, as we were going so far north, maybe we should wear our Arctic suits. But Per Thore just laughed and said that we would probably be happier in what we had been wearing for the last ten days. He obviously understood the climate a lot better than we did. We dismantled the tents, loaded our sleds and worked out what we would need in them when we got to Mageröya, the island on which Nordkapp lies. The rest of the kit could be put into the truck Ryno was driving.

Now came a new challenge, one that might well have defeated us. The dogs had just been put back into the trailer which was parked by the side of the road. We had camped some way from the road and in between the two was the swampland. It was hard enough pushing the heavy sleds across the snow, but now we had to push them over swamp and grassy tussocks and, this time, with no dogs to help. We pushed, pulled, tugged and said 'bother me' (or words to that effect) whereupon someone would eventually appear by our side like an angel and help get the sled over the next tussock and ultimately to the road. Once there, they had to be unloaded into the back of the truck and secured on top of the trailer. As soon as everything and everybody was safely in, we set off through the tunnels that connected the mainland to the islands, some of which took us 300 metres below sea level. I have travelled through many tunnels before but never known just how far below sea level I was – this felt really odd. They were like ordinary roads with lights but you had the curious feeling that above you was this ominous amount of water in a deserted landscape.

I can hear you asking why we, the dogs and the sleds were packed into a truck when we were meant to be opening a dog-sled trail. Well, the Gulf Stream, called the North Atlantic Drift up here, surrounds the islands and warms the sea. So there was no ice between the islands and much of the snow on the land was melting. It would have been absolutely impossible to have tried to sled through the tunnels – apart from anything else they are not that well lit. It would not have been right to stop on these very small islands, harness the dogs and sled for a short time, then unharness them and pack everything back into the truck to get to the next island. It would have been very confusing for the dogs. Frustrating as it was, it was just something we had to do. I noticed that there was a distinct lack of snow everywhere which started to make me somewhat apprehensive. In the past I have often kept my fears to myself but now, again, I decided to voice them. However, Per Thore was very reassuring and said that I would be fine. Wasn't that what he had said at the Kautokeino camp site? Maybe I should believe him this time.

Eventually, we crossed the little islands and arrived at a much bigger one, Magerōya, the last before the Arctic. My heart sank when I saw where we were to start sledding. There were lots of grassy tussocks and black jagged rocks but not very much snow. This certainly did not bode well. Per Thore again reassured me but I had a sense that this was still going to be very difficult, if not the most difficult part of the expedition. You know what they say: 'the longest mile is the last mile home.' Also, I was exhausted. The expedition had taken a lot out of me; and in fact, I was not alone: it had taken a lot out of Cathy as well and even the dogs were tired and reluctant to get out of the trailer. As I tried to get my lead dog, Vinga, out of the trailer she put her two front paws on the ridge for the door and refused to budge. I had to lift her paws over the ridge and literally manhandled her out. All of the dogs had to have bootees put on because of the condition of the ground. The website update read:

Modelling canine booties

The long days and tough snow conditions took their toll on the dogs' paws and by the last day most had booties on. The majority hate the booties and the two dogs here, Shara and Zita, Cathy's lead dogs, were expert at removing them by opening the velcro tabs with their front teeth.

Photo 50 – Do we have to sled? (see page 126)
At least this time the sleds were relatively empty. Well, I thought that that would be a bonus but in fact, with hindsight, perhaps it was a disadvantage. (Just how contrary can I get?) We set off and immediately my dogs got tangled in their lines; I untangled them and then they went all over the rocks and seemed to refuse to follow the path that Per Thore had taken. I was in a mess, tired, fed up and wanted this nightmare to be over. I was certainly not enjoying myself. One of my lead dogs, Sally, was so reluctant to be there that she kept turning round towards me instead of running forward. This made Vinga bite her to make her behave and I suddenly had visions of the fiasco we had had with my dogs biting each other as we arrived at Soppero – not again, I thought: I can't stand it. I hadn't slept well the previous night as it had been -20ºC and the snow where we had camped was very, very hard and uncomfortable. Now the fatigue was definitely beginning to tell.

Per Thore and Cathy were well ahead and waiting for me. As I appeared over the summit they were in the valley below. My dogs saw them and went straight over the grass tussocks and rocks. By then I had had enough. I was terrified, and let go of the sled. It went over. Exasperated, I walked up to it, picked it up resignedly and got on to sled down to them. Per Thore told me to keep up and Cathy shouted at me to keep to the right. When I looked to the left I realised why. There was a large hole under the snow. I knew my dogs had a habit of cutting corners so I was prepared for the worst. I just managed to skirt it, how I don't know, but the accomplishment raised my spirits and we raced on once more as a team.

The terrain continued to be very difficult as there was hardly any snow. There were grassy tussocks to navigate and, with one dog continually turning back, for me this was becoming a nightmare again. The website update read:

Rock dodgems

As we approached the coast (which is warmed by the Gulf stream) there was less and less snow, making for interesting navigation through the rocks and grass hummocks.

The expedition ran on dog food and coffee – the last coffee granules were shared out on the final morning. We couldn't afford to be out there another day!

We came to a stream which we had to cross. There was no alternative. Cathy's team of dogs stopped in front of the stream and refused to go forward and so mine came to a halt, confused as to what they should do. Cathy's dogs now turned back so I pushed mine on and Per Thore came back to help. Now it was a case of getting off the sled and, whilst Per Thore pulled the dogs through the ice-cold water, I waded across pushing the sled. Sally, my wayward lead dog who had decided she definitely did not want to run, had exasperated even Per Thore and was now deposited by him very unceremoniously in his sled, which made the going a little easier for me. She was somewhat reluctant, to say the least, to go into his sled but a few fine words from our leader and some very careful placement of straps and bindings and she sat like 'lady muck' securely in his sled until the end of the trail. (Although somewhat in disgrace with the other dogs!)

Photo 51 – Naughty Sally! (see page 127)

It was at times like this when I was tired, battered and bruised and everything was going haywire that I wondered why I was doing this at all. We then had to traverse a very steep incline with the sleds sliding down it sideways. It was terrifying, especially in the mood I was in. I felt that Per Thore was always reprimanding me and I was hot and bothered. Now I suddenly realised why Per Thore had said to us not to use the Arctic suits. This last part of the trail was extremely hard work: Cathy and I would have been roasted. However, thankfully, we were soon back in snow-covered mountains again and the sledding was a bit easier.

We were getting closer to the northernmost tip of Europe. This was the last land before the North Pole so it was a great tourist attraction for people from all over the world. Ryno's task now was to drive the trailer to trail end, the road to Nordkapp had only recently been opened and every so often the road came within view of where we were sledding. This was our only opportunity to get some photographs of all three of us sledding together. However, as Ryno came forward to take the photographs, the dogs saw him and then the trailer and would make a bee-line for it. I have to admit that I nearly did as well. But the end was in sight, the dogs were on track again and before us was a snow-covered mountain making the sledding easier and certainly a lot more relaxing after the terrain we had just encountered.

We sled on in perfect conditions for a while, and by now Per Thore and Cathy were quite far ahead and crossing the road where there was snow on both sides. They had done a more circuitous route to get to the bottom of the next mountain. I was watching where they were going so that we could try to catch up with them; but my dogs (we were now quite a long way behind) also saw what was happening and spied a chance of another shortcut. This entailed going down a fairly steep bank which, at that particular moment, was hidden from me. By now Per Thore and Cathy were directly in front of me but some

Photo 52 – So close now

way off. Having not seen the bank I was temporarily unbalanced but could have recovered if the dogs had not suddenly started to cross the road prematurely. My sled was slipping sideways and there was nothing I could do about it as the dogs disappeared over the edge and I was not concentrating hard enough – I did everything that was needed for a heavy sled but this was now a very light sled. I broke one of the marker posts, and really didn't stand a chance. I knew if I continued to hold on (as Per Thore had instructed) I was going to be flung onto some very sharp, jagged black rocks to my right and the first part of me to connect with them would be my head. Now, not wanting my head to be split open I made an executive decision – I let go. I jumped off in an act of self-preservation as we hit them, the sled went over onto its right-hand side and I landed in a heap on the ground. The dogs carried on their way dragging the sled along. However, they too were very tired which made it fairly easy for Per Thore to catch them. I picked myself up and slowly plodded towards them staring resolutely at my feet.

Per Thore was asking whether I was all right, whether I was hurt, but I could not answer – if I did I knew I would break down. I was exhausted. He asked me again 'How are you?' 'Fine' I sullenly replied. 'Did you hurt yourself?' 'Yes.' 'Are you all right?' 'Yes.' Then Per Thore did a near-fatal thing – he told me that I should use both brakes when sledding. I exploded and retorted that I knew how to sled but if the dogs had a will of their own there was nothing I could do about it. I ranted at him that one minute he was telling me to do one thing and the next something else. Cathy told me later that whilst I was venting my frustration Per Thore was suggesting that we discuss it later, but I had no idea what he was saying. I was just not in the mood to 'discuss' anything.

Having released all my pent-up emotions (poor Per Thore) my sense of humour returned and Per Thore gave me a great big bear hug which was exactly what I needed – empathy. Then he reunited me with my sled and my dogs. We were at a point where there were two options to get us to trail end and Per Thore asked me which way I wanted to go: straight on up the mountain or take an easier option. Both Per Thore and Cathy's sleds were pointing straight up the mountain which appeared to be the planned way and I wasn't going to change that. We raced up to the top to be met by two eagles circling high in the sky and Ryno with champagne and glasses!

Photo 53 – We made it! (see page 127)

All malevolence had vanished. We had made it. We'd achieved our goal. We'd done what the experienced mushers of Norway said couldn't be done. We'd opened a dog-sled trail to the northernmost tip of Europe. I was on top of the world – literally! I felt like the eagles soaring high above. All the pain, the frustration and the petty annoyances, everything that had felt bad about the route and that day disappeared in the knowledge that we had completed a route that had never been done before and which was thought to be impossible. We were jubilant. Tourists, who had made the journey by coach, came to take photographs of us with our ancient form of transport. They asked us (or rather Per Thore and Ryno as we did not speak the language) what we had been doing, where had we come from. Ahead lay the celebrations, a relaxing journey home by boat and the memories of accomplishing another goal. But, for the moment, it was a time to pause.

I watched with a smile on my face as the dogs, lying quietly on the snow, gradually took hold of the Velcro on the bootees in their mouth and peeled it open, one by one taking their bootees off as if to say 'Look what we have achieved. With all these cameras around, you really can't expect us to be wearing bootees!' Amazing characters! Once we had completed taking our own photographs (Ryno was working very hard as our 'professional photographer'), we turned our sleds in the direction of the trailer, leaving a pile of bootees where our dogs had been. One tourist very kindly returned them all to us. My dogs were in a tangle again so I put the ice anchor in, sorted them out and we set off again, only this time, as I neared Per Thore with a big smile on my face, I raised my arm in victory. The website update read:

Time to head home

Rona turns her sled away from the ocean that lies beyond Nordkapp.
It is time to head for home.

Photo 54 – I did it! (see page 128)

A little later, as one by one we unharnessed the dogs and struggled to hold on to them as we crossed the slippery ice to the trailer, I apologised to Per Thore. I had not wanted to lose my temper with him, I said, but at that moment it seemed that he was always having a go at me and never at Cathy. He told me that he often had a go at her, gave me another hug and a kiss and we were back in our old friendly relationship again. With all the dogs safely in the trailer, or so we thought, we set off to find our hotel. Ryno stopped the truck looking really worried as one of the doors to the trailer was open and one cage was empty, but we could see no dogs anywhere. He counted the dogs: we had them all but somehow we had managed to leave one cage free and put two dogs into one cage – who could that have been? He drove us to the hotel where we had a very welcome shower and a great meal. Then we packed our kit as we were taking only the bare necessities on the boat and gave our bags to the guys to put into the truck, before sinking into a very, very welcome comfortable bed. The following day it would be a 5 a.m. start to catch the steamer back to Tromsø.

Poor Ryno, he definitely had the worst job. Whilst we relaxed on the steamer home through the stunningly picturesque islands and fjords on the coast of Norway, he had to feed the dogs and drive ten hours back to Tromsø. Once there, he then had to put the dogs back into their kennels and feed them – and he hadn't even taken part in an expedition he would dearly have loved to have been on. But he was still part of the team – without him we would not have been able to accomplish our goal.

By 5.30 a.m. we were dressed and back in the hotel reception – to collect our takeaway breakfast. The three of us walked round to the steamer and settled into some decent seats so that we could see where we were going as well as where we had been sledding up in the mountains. The steamer headed south-west through all the islands off the coast and some breathtakingly beautiful scenery with the last of the winter snow clinging to the mountains by the sea. But, although it was lovely and relaxing, it was not nearly as exciting as being up in the mountains away from everyone and everything. (Some memories can be very short!) Although the day was overcast, every so often the sun peeked through the clouds and lit the mountain tops, making them look very tempting. Through my mind kept running thoughts of how I would love to be back up on the mountain sledding again. Just how contrary can I be? We sat drinking in the scenery for some time until Per Thore fell asleep, Cathy decided to update the website and I continued my writing.

The dispatch sent from the steamer was:

> At 13.50 European time, the Nordkapp Expedition reached its objective. Three tired mushers and 26 tired dogs (one so tired she was given a lift in a sled) arrived at the northern-most point of Europe, the Nordkapp. We cracked open a bottle of champagne and celebrated the successful conclusion to 11 days of travelling. It has to be said that the wilderness is not what it once was and we were greeted by a Visitors' Centre and a coach-load of tourists all frantically photographing the dogs. Nevertheless, we could look out over the deep blue sea, lying calm under stormy grey skies, and know that nothing lay between us and the North Pole.

It was a welcome time out on the steamer, a chance to take stock, reassess and just to relax before we were back in the throes of everyday life again. Dinner that evening was booked and there would be time for tea beforehand – very civilised, after days of not knowing when we were going to eat. The steamer docked in Tromsø very late in the evening and we took a taxi to Per Thore's. The dogs were so tired that there was no sound as we came up the drive. Usually they would have started barking but tonight they slept. Hege was there to greet us, with the smell of freshly baked bread wafting through the house and after a short chat and a drink we all went to bed, tired but happy to sleep the sleep of the victors.

Yes, we all just about made it in one piece although I did have doubts about myself especially on the last day. I was somewhat battered and bruised and would be sporting a scar for a while yet. When I tried to move I realised that I was full of aches and pains. If I turned my head, the muscles cried out and I found other muscles I didn't even know I had. The inside of my elbow hurt, and my shoulders, my legs were bruised, my fingers hurt – all pains that would pass but the memories would linger on. I made another mental note not to go to the doctor just yet for a check up – I would not pass. I think that maybe I am not a natural dog-sledder; but being out in the wilderness with these incredible animals in such a beautiful landscape is something that has to be experienced.

It took several cups of strong, black coffee to get us all going in the morning and, once breakfast was out of the way, it was time to unload the truck and get all the equipment sorted. Whilst Per Thore took the sleds and dog equipment, I took the sleeping bags, food and our luggage and put them away as best as I could. Meanwhile Cathy sat inside downloading pictures off the iPod enhancing the colour and preparing them for Per Thore and me. This was also the first opportunity Per Thore and I would have to see what had been put onto the website whilst we had been sledding.

Later that day, whilst Hege and Per Thore went to visit friends, Cathy and I decided to explore the island. We borrowed Hege's car and with the naiveté of foreigners, set off without a map thinking there must be a road going all the way round this island we were on. How wrong can you be? Had we learnt nothing in the last eleven days? The scenery as we came round each corner made us catch our breath but how to drive round the island defeated us. Every so often as we drove along the coast roads, they would just finish in the middle of nowhere and we would have to backtrack. We had no idea where we were or how to get back. This was a totally different type of adventure. Soon we were reduced to fits of laughter, tears streaming down our faces, as time and time again we came to a dead end. Eventually, considerably later than expected, and after we had received a phone call from Per Thore asking if we were all right, we arrived back home. Hege looked after us really well and Saturday was a day of celebratory meals and relaxation before Per Thore was to take us to the airport the following day.

The final website dispatch read:

> Goodbye and happy travels. The dogs are back in their kennels, taking a well-deserved rest and lots of food. Rona and Cathy are flying back to the UK this afternoon. All that remains of the expedition is a line of sled tracks stretching across 532 kilometres

of snow, and some four million paw prints from the dogs, gradually melting away in the spring sunshine.

It had been the most incredible experience.

Photo 55 — Sally and Vinga — we're off (see page 128)

APPENDIX 1

Arctic Leadership Challenges

As I started to write about this expedition, one of those 'of course' moments flashed through my mind. I've done some very diverse 'expeditions' – racing a yacht the wrong way round the world on the BT Global Challenge Round the World Yacht Race in 2000–1, trekking with bears and cougars and now opening a thought-to-be-impossible dog-sled trail to the northernmost tip of Europe; and there were others. It dawned on me that on each one I had learnt many lessons about leadership and teamwork as well as how to achieve your goals by thinking differently.

I rang Per Thore and said 'I've got an idea of how we can work together'. I shared my idea with him and he said 'I think that is a great idea. Did you know that I also have a yacht so we could take them sailing in the summer?' So the Arctic Leadership Challenges were born.

The **Arctic Leadership Challenges for Corporates** take groups into the Arctic Circle (land-based not on the sea ice), dog-sledding in the winter and sailing in the summer for professional development. Participants are put through a variety of experiences to accelerate their learning on leadership and teamwork and also how to think differently to achieve their goals.

The **Arctic Leadership Challenges for Universities** take university students into the Arctic Circle (land-based not on the sea ice), dog-sledding in the winter and trekking in Svalbard in the summer. They will also undertake experiential learning on leadership and teamwork as well as how to think differently to achieve their goals, thus giving them a head start in the world of business.

The **Arctic Leadership Challenges for Schools** take Sixth Form pupils into the Arctic Circle (land-based not on the sea ice), dog-sledding in the winter and trekking in Svalbard in the summer. The pupils also undertake experiential learning about leadership and teamwork and how to think differently to achieve their goals – which will help them get the edge on others wanting to go to university, take up an apprenticeship or go straight into the world of business.

APPENDIX 2

The Charity Challenge for Cancer Research UK

Part 1 — An Idea is Born

I bumped into an excited Heidi Kurtz in Oxford who said she was going to raise money for Cancer Research UK, for which the reward was dog-sledding in Lapland. She explained what it entailed and it sounded fantastic. I could not get the idea out of my mind – it just buzzed around sending sparks of excitement through me. I thought about it all the way home. As soon as I got in I called Cancer Research UK and put my name down. A few days later, a bulky envelope landed on my doormat and I dropped everything to read the contents. My heart sank – it seemed impossible to raise the required £3,000. Fundraising was not my forte and filled me with dread; but if I wanted to go dog-sledding, I would have to rise to the challenge.

Having taken part in several adventures (racing a yacht the wrong way round the world and trekking in Canada) I had decided to set up my own business helping others achieve their goals; but it can take a long time to become financially secure. Sometimes we just have to be flexible when 'push comes to shove' and my bank account told me that time was now. I applied for some temporary positions and was eventually persuaded to take a job which was a 30-minute drive away. The money was good so my business would have to go on hold.

Realising Heidi regretted having divulged her plans to me, we agreed that I would go on a different week from her and wouldn't approach the people she wanted to sponsor her. I completed the application form, signed on the dotted line and put it with my cheque into the post. I was committed! Now came the hard part – to raise the money. I had no choice. It was either raise the money or lose my deposit, and I certainly did not want to do that; having been 'out of work' for two years of adventuring, my bank balance was very unhealthy. Maybe it was a lack of self-confidence which caused the mental block as to how to start raising money but I couldn't find any enthusiasm, let alone ideas, despite the list Cancer Research UK had sent. It was going to be a slow, steady plod for me, writing lots of letters to everyone I knew and hoping that they would want to support such a good cause. Having been brought up to believe that 'it's better to give than to receive', I didn't enjoy asking. However, one by one the cheques started to trickle in. I even wrote to my local supermarket to ask whether I could make a collection outside their building at Christmas, but all the days had been allocated a year earlier so I was relegated to the end of January.

Although I had raised money for various charities before, this was turning into a real eye-opener for me: there is a whole industry based on raising money for good causes. It was an experience in itself.

I stood outside the supermarket on a cold day in January wearing my banner and holding my bucket, both clearly emblazoned with the words 'Cancer Research UK', as the shoppers wheeled their trolleys laden with food to their cars. Some would stop and give me some money with a smile; others would push their trolley straight at me, realise I was asking for money and duck away at the last moment as though I didn't exist; some would even push their trolley all the way to the car, load up the car and then walk back saying 'I couldn't go without giving'. No matter what, I didn't mind, every little bit helped and I was extremely grateful.

The deadline drew nearer and I was a desperately long way from the target. Fearing that I would miss the goal, I racked my brains for new ideas. Just when I thought I was going to fail someone at work suggested speaking to the company as, unbeknown to me, they had a policy of matching charity sponsorship pound for pound. Tentatively I asked whether they would support me. As it was a good cause they agreed, providing I raised a further £250. You know when you think you have exhausted every avenue and are asked to raise some more it is the hardest thing going. But the end goal – dog-sledding inside the Arctic Circle – was the incentive to do just that. Digging deep I found other ideas and gradually the amount crept up and I made it. The company made their contribution but there was a small shortfall. I re-read the literature again and telephoned Claire, the event organiser. It was agreed that as I was so close I could go and pay the rest on my return. At least I was going – I was ecstatic! Now I just had to get fit.

Our flights were booked for Sunday 16 March 2003. On the previous Friday I felt depressed, I was tired, hungry and very apprehensive. I am not a skier and slippery surfaces scare me. I must have sounded really dejected when I called my sister – who is a tremendous supporter of what I do. Back in January, Cancer Research UK had held a meeting in London to inform us about the trek and what we would need to take with us. This was just what I needed to prepare properly but where had I been? I was on a survival weekend on the South Coast in preparation for the Fastnet Race in August. However, they had sent us a list of the other participants and in a fit of desperation I telephoned Sue, who was also on the Challenge and quizzed her about what to expect. We talked for ages – she was chatty and articulate and shared the information, allaying my fears. I had already interrogated Claire when she joined us on a training trail in Derby. I was gradually getting a good idea of what was required. Would I be right? That would only be revealed during the Challenge.

From past adventures I was used to taking only the minimum of clothing – if it was not in the bag I would do without. Our rucksacks were only allowed to weigh 15 kilos so extras were not an option. Slowly, oh so slowly, over that final weekend I was getting excited again. What I really needed was to make some serious money so that I could follow my heart. My brain was slowly revving up for overload. I was off on an adventure and more ideas were springing into my head as I prepared.

Saturday dawned. One of those busy days getting all the last-minute bits and pieces dealt with ensued. My head torch hadn't worked properly since my last adventure and, as usual, I had left it to the very last moment to get it checked. There was a loose connection so it needed to be repaired: I would have to buy a new one. It was to get worse. I had not checked the new head torch properly until I was packing in the evening. I have loads of batteries at home. I buy them thinking I haven't any and then they pop up in every drawer in the house. But just my luck, this head-torch needed a very different type of battery. It was far too late to search for one in the shops now and I convinced

Photo 56 – Rona ready to sled

myself that I would be able to buy one at Heathrow, so I put it out of my mind.

I called my children to say I was off. 'Where to?' asked Nicola, my daughter. 'The Arctic' I replied. 'Oh, have a good time' was her response. Well, at least she wasn't going to worry!

We met at Heathrow and very soon I started to work out who was who amongst my sledding companions. The majority seemed to have done several challenges before and, of the twelve, I think only Sophie, Paul, Sue and I were virgin Charity Challengers. I wondered how the others managed to raise the money so frequently; but they were committed charity supporters. It seemed they spent a considerable amount of time raising money and their reward was to put themselves through some extremely arduous challenges, walking along the Yangtse River, trekking in Peru, walking to Everest Base Camp and many more. It was interesting to find out everyone's story: Andru was on her seventh challenge, Moira her fifth. How did they do it?

We arrived at Kiruna, in Norway, to find the local people going about their business wrapped in more appropriate attire than these interlopers from 2,500 kilometres to the south. We piled into two vehicles and were driven through this alien landscape to the starting point for the challenge – the Musher's Lodge, run by Taisto, a man of few words, but memorable for his stature. The lodge looked like an ordinary house half-buried under the snow – surely we couldn't all fit into it. Like a Tardis, once inside it seemed to go on forever. Everywhere there were utilitarian dormitories – it was used to wave upon wave of new recruits arriving and then moving on using this traditional mode of transport before returning and departing, maybe forever. Outside everywhere we looked there were the huskies: Taisto's four-legged partners barked a welcome – or was it a warning? Everywhere there were dogs either in large cages or tethered to trees. We dumped our bags in the dormitories and went to greet them – the power for our transport for the next week.

After our evening meal, we had a comprehensive briefing interspersed with the howling of the huskies. Our leader was Sid (real name Steve), a firm, serious man with the weight of responsibility of leading twelve volunteers weighing heavily on his shoulders. Digger, the Doctor, was also serious but with a more light-hearted side trying to break through – I think he was also hoping to be superfluous. Then there was Per Thore, our guide, a man who watched and assessed. He used few words but had an air of total confidence about him. At this point they were but names. Soon we would come to know them – and ourselves – a lot better. Each explained their part in precisely how we would operate. Once they had finished we headed back to the dormitories and slumped into our beds completely shattered.

At 3 a.m. something must have walked through the kennels as the dogs created an unearthly din, howling and barking. We would get used to this nocturnal activity but right now, needless to say, we all awoke and there was a steady procession to the bathroom. In the morning, after breakfast, we collected our Arctic suits, gloves, hats and boots from the equipment room. It seemed to take ages until we all had the right sizes.

Once suitably kitted out, we ventured outside to learn how to put on a dog harness, attach the dogs to the sleds and have our one-and-only lesson on sledding! The previous evening, the dogs had been very excited and looked quite scary but once we started to handle them, although still excited, they appeared really tame and friendly. It was only much later on that I would find out just how vicious they could be.

After lunch we set off racing down the track, with Taisto watching that we took care of his dogs, and then turned into the forest. Coming out of the forest we went down a steep slope onto a frozen lake. We crossed the lake and went back into the forest. Eventually we arrived at the Wilderness Lodge at Vékérééjarvi having covered 15 kilometres. We were now in an area where the Sámi people live. We unharnessed the dogs and settled ourselves into the lodge for the night.

The scenery here was spectacular; the lodge was beside a frozen lake surrounded by birch trees and mountains. I could have happily stayed there for a long time just writing, the place had such a wonderful feeling about it. I was standing by the bridge taking in the scenery when something caught my eye. It was quite incongruous – pushing their way out of the snow by the edge of the lake were the hulls of two canoes. But with the jobs done and photos taken it was back to the lodge and, leaving the guys to finish off preparing the meal, we girls took the opportunity of having a quick sauna. We were back just in time to devour a very welcome meal of reindeer meat with chopped vegetables in a sauce. We sat around the candlelit cabin laughing and chatting about the thrills and spills of that first day before heading gratefully for bed. The guys decided it was now time for their sauna; but they wanted do it the traditional way and so after the heat of the sauna they rushed out naked into the snow.

It was de rigeur before bed to leave the cabin and head for the wood shack that contained the toilet. When I say 'contained the toilet' this, in fact, was a wooden plank with a large hole in it suspended across from one side of the hut to the other on which you would sit. Rather than creep out in the middle of the night, I decided to make a hopefully final visit before going to bed. In the semi-darkness I left the main cabin and made my way towards the toilet shack only to be confronted by the sight of all the males from the group standing naked in the snow outside the sauna. Averting one's eyes was not an option if one did not want to fall over but the sight of so many shapes, sizes and dimensions of man was distracting to say the least. I was quite relieved in many ways to return to the sanctuary of the main cabin and climb into bed for a well-earned sleep.

As morning dawned we were told there was a storm coming through so we had to set off as soon as possible. Down the track we stopped sledding for a moment: this time it was Digger who was concentrating on taking some photos, so he didn't notice that those in front of him had started to move off again. Major point: always keep hold of your sled, a lesson I had already quickly learned. One more photo and Digger's dogs were off – but without him. He went headlong into the snow dropping his camera whilst Sue videoed it all including his long, solitary plodding walk to catch up with his sled. This little incident would later become ammunition to enable Sid to rib Digger.

Photo 57 – Cooking en route (see page 129)

Moving off again through the forest the track suddenly opened into a clearing just as Per Nils, a friend of Per Thore's, arrived by snowmobile. It was lunch time so Per Thore cut down some branches to make a fire on top of a very large stone and proceeded to cook soup for us to which he added some reindeer meat. Meanwhile Sid was busy using an axe on some frozen reindeer meat so that we could feed the dogs. There was half a kilo for each dog and we were given strict instructions to toss it to them – apparently this meant there was less chance of us losing our fingers! Whilst we were eating our lunch, one team of dogs managed to free its ice anchor and took off. Sid was in the midst of ribbing Digger about losing his sled earlier when Per Thore suddenly jumped on Per Nils' snowmobile and chased after the dogs who, attached to Sid's sled, were heading back to the Wilderness Lodge. Now the tables were turned and it was Digger's opportunity to rib Sid. We had a long leisurely lunch, to give the dogs a chance to eat and rest before we set off once again.

We eventually arrived at yet another frozen river where the snow covering the ice was at least ten centimetres deep but in various exposed places we could see it was melting. As we rounded a corner there was a large footprint in the snow and that night the discussions were on whether it had been made by a wolverine; Per Nils thought that it had. It gradually got colder and colder and started to rain. I just had to put on my jacket, which became a work of art in the conditions we now encountered. Not only that but it took some considerable time to accomplish and within a few minutes of my success the rain stopped, the sun came out again and – you've guessed it – I was getting too hot. So the whole process had to be reversed until the jacket was folded and wedged onto the sled again. However, at least I accomplished it all without falling off a moving sled!

Towards the end of that day's sledding we raced down a hill and onto yet another frozen river. These rivers were everywhere, making some great roads for us to travel along. However, this one was in quite open countryside and we were totally unprotected. We were blown to the edge of the river where the snow was deep and soft. The wind was incredibly strong and the wind chill had now dropped to -20°C. It was unbelievably difficult to sled and there was nothing we could do to stop the sleds slipping on the icy snow. Even the dogs were being blown backwards and no matter what we did we couldn't prevent the sleds from being blown to the side of the river by the wind. We were out of control.

With sleds stopping and starting we all got mixed up with each other and my dogs were biting each other trying to release their legs from the now tightened gangline. It took some time to straighten everyone out and get them onto the bank where we were to stay for the night. Once everyone was there, first aid was administered to my dogs then we went off in search of our beds for the night, in the loft of a large house.

Part 2 — Sledding to Soppero and beyond

Having established where we were to sleep we were given a night off from our usual duties as our meal was to be cooked for us. We quickly returned to the ground floor and entered the large room where it was to be served – we were very hungry. In one corner there was a built-in old iron cooker and, round the corner, a fire was alight in a cavity two feet off the floor. Nestling by its side was a big pot of hot coffee. Brit Marie and Per Nils owned the buildings; both were Sámi and followed the reindeer in true nomadic style. Brit Marie was cooking us an amazing dinner, a typical Sámi meal with reindeer meat. Although this was not the first time we had savoured reindeer meat it was certainly very different from our previous experience and quite delicious.

Once the meal was over we all sat around listening to Brit Marie as she recounted tales of life as a Sámi after which Per Nils ushered us outside into the cold to feed the wild reindeer in their enclosure. Next to their pen, down nearer to the river in a very exposed position, we noticed a small building with a very steep sloping roof made with wooden slats between which were large gaps: it was the toilet. From time to time the snow drifted through the gaps making the wooden plank somewhat treacherous to sit on. Once the reindeer were fed we all made use of the little hut, trying hard not to get frozen to the 'seat' before returning to our dormitory and settling ourselves down to sleep. The next morning the weather was atrocious and it looked ominously as though we would not be able to sled up the mountain to Jarmé.

Back in England when we were training on a trek across the Dales, Claire had reminisced about her visit to Jarmé and how after a sauna everyone had to run outside and jump into a large hole in the ice! She was insistent that we should all take the plunge – literally. Tucked into the darkest recesses of my rucksack was my swimsuit. Yes, I know you're meant to be naked but there are only so many challenges that one can cope with at a time and naked, in public and freezing water, amounted to one too many.

By now the temperature was -9°C and the wind-chill was -20° to -30°C; we were in the middle of a white out. With breakfast over Sid told us the bad news: we wouldn't be sledding that day. There was a real danger of frostbite and of losing people (literally having people die through losing their way in the white out) if we tried to go up the mountain to Jarmé, especially as we would be sledding straight into the teeth of the storm. Disappointed, we didn't really believe that it was that bad, so Per Nils told the dissenters (Ian, Lucy and I) to walk down to the river to check the wind. Outside we had to fight our way against the conditions and I have to admit I only got as far as the sauna. The wind was so cold and strong it was burning our cheeks. Where we had chained the dogs all we could see were little mounds of snow. We could hardly see where anything was. Reluctantly we had to agree that just maybe they were right and it was best to stay put.

We got back to the house and explained there were no dogs to be seen only mounds of snow at intervals along the chains. Per Thore explained that the dogs curl up into tight balls with their noses tucked under their tails to protect their stomachs from the freezing temperatures and that's how they stayed all night. To move meant losing heat which was the last thing they would want in these temperatures.

Photo 60 – Per Nils in Sámi clothes (see page 130)

However, Per Nils had come to breakfast that morning wearing traditional Sámi reindeer chaps. A great photo opportunity! Brit Marie and Per Nils had established a museum on the Sámi culture in an outbuilding and once breakfast was over Brit Marie took us round explaining how the exhibits were used in real life and how the Sámi people lived. We all tried our skill at lassoing a reindeer – in reality, it was a pair of antlers on a stick. It was hilarious, with great shouts of glee if anyone actually succeeded. Per Thore went down to check Pria's paw, which was swollen: at least a day without sledding gave it a chance to heal, but the next day we would have to leave whatever the weather.

Whilst Sue interviewed Digger and Sid for her video, I joined Per Thore as he fed the dogs. Digger the Doc was a great guy: good fun, amiable and much loved by us all, he was so easy going. He was one of those guys who was quietly comfortable with himself and just enjoyed life. I think we all enjoyed just having him around. Sid, on the other hand, took his role very seriously (as, in a medical crisis, Digger would certainly also have done) and would drill into us what we should and should not do. It was really to ensure our safety, obviously a very important part of his job; but it often came across very

Photo 58 — At last, we're sledding again

differently from the way I think he intended. However, at the end of the day, it was his responsibility to keep all of us safe.

Photo 59 — The turf house (see page 129)

Next to the sauna was a turf house, typical of the sort of building where Nomads would live. Apparently, whenever Per Thore visited Soppero, this was where he stayed. He loved it, feeling more at home in the turf house than in the bigger buildings. I asked whether he would mind if I took a look around. He told me to go ahead. There was only one storey and the inside was amazing: the walls and roof were made from slender tree trunks (they are no thicker than your wrist, the only size which can grow this far north) and everything was made of wood; inside it was surprisingly spacious. A roaring wood burner kept it very cosy. Outside all the walls and roof were covered with turf, hence the name.

Venturing back outside I found Per Nils working with a wild reindeer which he was trying to break in by sheer perseverance. He managed to get a harness on it for the first time and attach it to a sleigh. But it wasn't happy and he had problems controlling it so he suddenly jumped on the sleigh and they were off down the road in a flash with Per Nils waving as he disappeared. I think the reindeer may have bolted – if reindeer bolt! There was obviously some sort of mishap along the way because not long afterwards he returned walking along the road holding the rope attached to the reindeer and pulling the sleigh himself. Then he offered one of the guys a ride – an offer which was enthusiastically accepted, but first the volunteer had to catch his own reindeer! He seemed to take ages failing in his attempts to lasso a reindeer and the herd scattered around the pen each time the lasso was thrown. That was until Per Thore joined in. Their patience was incredible as they waited, watched and then attempted to lasso one; but suddenly, with a little run, Per Thore threw the lasso and caught a reindeer by his hind foot. With a bit of a slide across the frozen snow Per Thore held on and Per Nils walked hand over hand along the rope until he came to the reindeer; turning it on its side, he put a bridle on. But a second one had to be caught and then both were harnessed to the sleigh. With Per Nils holding the rope and our fellow sledder languishing on the back they set off at high speed. Shortly the sleigh and Per Nils reappeared at relatively high speed but without his companion – he was later seen walking slowly back along the road!

The following day we were to start our return journey but that night we had the most incredible experience of seeing a full-blown Northern Lights fantasia! We watched until they faded away even though the temperature outside had risen to -15°C.

In the morning, with bags packed and breakfast cleared, we went in search of our sleds. When we first arrived we had put the ice anchors into soft snow to stop the sleds being blown away in the strong winds. Now they were firmly frozen into the snow lurking beneath the soft new layer deposited overnight and we needed the axe to chip them out. I had a feeling that leaving Soppero might be more chaotic than our arrival – it was on a hill, the new snow was soft and now even deeper and the dogs had had a day off so were very lively. We were supposed to stay in the same order in the train, so I quickly harnessed my dogs and worked out when I should start. Luckily after Per Thore's final inspection, Pria was confirmed fit to work. However, because of the way the dog chains had originally been set out, when the time came to set off all the sleds were scattered throughout the trees. Per Thore set off but only a few went after him, so concerned were they that everyone should be in the correct order. Moira set off and then stopped; I followed but again couldn't go anywhere. Pandemonium reigned. Per Thore stopped in the middle of the river to wait for us and looked back at the mayhem. One by one some of us joined him but most didn't – Carol's dogs had gone lame. Just to add to the chaos, the National Dog-sled Champion had turned up to watch us leave. I wondered what he thought. Eventually we all made it to the middle of the river and off we went.

Having missed our opportunity to sled up to Jarmé, we were now on our homeward journey retracing some of our steps and skirting round the mountain to pick up the trail later on. It was freezing as we sled along the exposed river but soon we were in the shelter of the forest. Suddenly we came to an abrupt standstill for no apparent reason: there was Per Thore walking meaningfully towards me. I thought I might have been doing something wrong but he just wanted to know how my two dogs were fairing after their injuries. I had spent most of my time since we set off watching them carefully so was able to report that they were coping well. Satisfied, Per Thore returned to his sled and we set off once more. It was not long after this that I had my encounter with a tree and did my own impression of a horizontal Superman.

Whilst Per Thore built the fire to boil water for our lunch, Sid lodged a complaint. He didn't think we were being fair to the dogs, the snow was soft and when we were going uphill he felt we should be mushing more than we were. Mushing is when you have one foot on the runner and one foot scooting along on the snow – it's a little like skateboarding. Most of my time was spent braking as Moira's dogs were slower than mine. Sid felt I should still mush but whenever I did the gangline went slack and I was afraid that I would catch Pria's leg again. As soon as I took my foot off the brake, the dogs were so pleased that they raced on and I had to brake quickly or go into Moira. Quietly Paul agreed with me that I couldn't mush as it would have been too confusing for the dogs. However, Sid was so upset we all mushed and mushed, going so fast that we arrived at Esrange, our next destination, earlier than anticipated.

In fact, we arrived there in chaos as we tried to avoid trees and snow ridges; we finally came to a halt amongst four differently sized wooden buildings. Our sleeping and eating cabin was tiny but the toilet cabin had two toilets with the luxury of polystyrene seats! The sauna cabin was back towards the lake and retracing our steps onto the lake there was a stack some distance from the edge of the forest – this signified our ice-hole where we could collect drinking water which had a very peaty taste!

Our group's assigned duty this time was to feed the dogs. The five of us began to fetch water for the boiler from the ice-hole, carrying it up the hill through the forest to the boiler hut whilst Per Thore chopped enough frozen meat for the dogs' soup. But it took time for the water for the soup to boil and my fellow 'dog patrol' sledders gradually disappeared. I thought they would return. However, I ended up feeding the seventy dogs myself; putting the bowls down, ladling the soup into them, then collecting the empty bowls, moving them on to the next set of hungry dogs and ladling out more soup for them. This was the moment that would make a big change in my life. Per Thore came out of his cabin and asked:

'Where are the rest of them?'

'I don't know.'

'So you are feeding the dogs on your own?'

'Well yes, I suppose I am.'

'Oh! I will take you on an expedition anytime.'

He then came and helped me. Little did I realise at the time that within twelve months those words would become a reality. My heart gave a little flutter of excitement.

I had lost track of time and had totally forgotten that it was Easter; our dinner that night started with a drink of rum and apple juice produced by Moira who then distributed Easter eggs for dessert. The guys did the washing up whilst we went for a sauna, then we relaxed in the cabin whilst the guys had theirs. With all of us in the cabin it was an interesting exercise watching the fiasco as everyone either wanted to or did not want to go to bed with some element of decorum. However, our resident jokers kept the temperature even, most of the time. We managed to pack all of us into bed in the cabin, although it was a challenge getting out of the cabin during the night if you wanted to go to the toilet!

It was -16ºC the next morning. Chaos reigned as we packed the sleds and harnessed the dogs. Starting any morning is difficult but today we would be leaving the cabins in two different groups going in different directions to join up on the lake as one train in our usual positions. This was going to be interesting and I watched and waited. Per Thore appeared from his cabin and the dogs started a frenzied barking; and as he got to his sled, untied the safety line and removed his anchor, they all came into line.

The other group were to go first, so we watched in expectation. There was a rush, a flurry, some shouts and they were off. They appeared round the corner and came to an orderly halt a little way from our exit. Releasing the brakes we now moved off. The dogs set off like bullets; it was always the hardest moment of the day as the dogs race to keep up with their master.

Racing out of the forest and round a bend in thick snow is difficult; but filming at the same time is well-nigh impossible for novices like us. Sue was trying to film the challenge and her sled went over – but by and large for a group like ours we did well, although it was the end of Sue's film. Maddy also had a tricky time but once we were all back on our sleds we could proceed again at quite a fast pace along a twisting frozen river.

We came to a halt. A message came down the line to be quiet and keep a firm hold of the dogs and, in front of us a little further along the river, a small herd of reindeer timidly came out of the forest, slowly crossed in front of us and bolted up the far bank, disappearing into the forest again as quickly as they could.

On we went again, the pace much faster than before. Was this because we were now getting the hang of sledding or a time constraint? I do not know and it was not important. It was exhilarating and scary at the same time. I had only been skiing once when I was 15 years old and racing over this icy terrain pulled by four energetic and very enthusiastic dogs was for me very frightening. I think I was meant to be in control of the dogs but it certainly didn't always feel like that.

We raced on along rivers, through small parts of the forest and then suddenly we were out on another enormous frozen lake. We must have looked good from the side – a vision we were never able to capture – as fifteen dog teams raced across this great wilderness. However, now there was a moment to look at the scenery – snow-capped mountains nestling behind the hills surrounding the lake. As we sled along there was also time to think and reflect without interruptions. It occurred to me that this blanket of snow meant I had no conception of how far or near we were to civilisation. At Soppero we knew we were on the outskirts of a village as Brit Marie had taken us in and shown us a local hostel which was, innovatively, also both an hotel and a church; a pleasant place for contemplation.

However, this day I was totally unprepared for the sight that came into view as we rounded a bend. Off to our left were two women wearing crash helmets, warm jackets and long skirts which finished just above their ice-skating boots. The two of them were enjoying themselves on a relatively small piece of ice doing figures of eight and re-creating a bizarre picture of old – holding out their hands to each other one foot on the ice and one foot pushed out behind they looked as though they came from an age gone by – except for the crash helmets! Suddenly we swerved off to the right just behind what looked like grasses coming through the snow. On again round a sharp right hand turn took us back into the perils of the forest once again.

We were heading for home and I think the dogs knew it: their top speed was 16 kph. Soon we found ourselves on another massive lake but this one was very slippery. To our right, igloos came into view then the Ice Palace, opposite which were a number of men working with large mechanical vehicles. They were digging huge lumps of ice out of the lake and transporting them across to an area by the Ice Palace. The blocks were crystal clear. Apparently as the river was very fast running these huge blocks of ice were exported round the world to be made into ice sculptures.

There were some ice sculptures on the lake but we didn't have time to stay long. Off we went in no particular order and I suddenly realised that this was where, for me, the really scary part began. At the start of the trail during the briefing there had been mention of us racing each other on the way home. We lined up on the ice and the race began. I was hemmed in and my dogs had worked so hard to get next to Moira that when I let them go and they drew level with Moira's sled they were content and did not even try to go past her sled. At the end of the race there was chaos as we all arrived at the same point at the same time where we had to turn to the left and go up a narrow trail on a steep hill to a few houses.

Having sorted ourselves out, we arrived at the top and came to an abrupt halt. I thought we had arrived home but this was definitely not the Musher's Lodge. We had been briefed that we would not be stopping for lunch but then Per Thore told us to anchor the dogs. Sid gathered us together and told us to find our own space to contemplate why we were there and what we felt were our reasons for doing the challenge. He told us he wanted total silence while we thought about this and then he handed out the sandwiches – which all seemed a little incongruous.

I walked off to a little area where I could see a little yellow house with a cap for a chimney and to the left the basis for a wigwam. My reason for the challenge had been that I thought dog-sledding in the Arctic Circle sounded very romantic and exciting; and maybe that was the place where I was in my life at the time. Of course, the cause was a good one but it was only part of the reason why I was there. For some reason I became very emotional – maybe because I was tired and scared or because I was really thinking about my mother-in-law and my mother who had both died of cancer a few years earlier, I don't know. This was a very private moment and we did not share our thoughts with each other. Then I saw them, two lead dogs walking through the snow investigating the area. Well, that wasn't right. I managed to get them and holding on to their collar called Sid. His response was somewhat abrupt:

'What do you want?'

'I have two dogs here that have got free. I think we need Per Thore.'

He went off to find him whilst I took the dogs back to Maddy's team where Per Thore appeared and made the harness secure. He turned and looking now at my dogs asked;

'Whose team is this?'

'Mine,' I responded.

Domni's collar was hanging on the end of the line that joins the two lead dogs but Domni, although still harnessed, was not connected. We rectified the situation and then returned to our own thoughts.

Soon the moment was over and Per Thore helped everyone to remove the anchors where they were stuck in the deep snow. The dogs perked up as soon as he got onto his own sled and as he undid the safety line all the dogs stood to attention with tails in the air like banners, ready to run. We set off towards a road but this time as we turned the corner we saw there was a tunnel so we could sled underneath it, although it would mean that we had a choice either to squat down very low or lose the top half of our bodies. Squatting seemed the best option. Before we knew what was happening we were on a winding path at the top of a hill, a very steep hill. Worse still, Per Thore had decided to go down it!

Homeward bound and the dogs running flat out, we spiralled down the mountain with one runner hanging in mid-air for most of the time; but at the end the trail was just a sheer drop followed by a couple of mogul-like bumps. I wondered whether Per Thore enjoyed testing us to the limit or was just enjoying himself as we went along. I am no skier and I was terrified but worse was to come. At least when we were on snow I could temper the speed by my use of the brake and by the sheer fact that I did not get off the sled and run with the dogs when the snow was either soft or we went uphill. I think Moira was grateful for that at least. My dogs' noses were touching her most of the time which must have been very annoying. If I tried to hold them back I was told to keep close to the person in front. If I took my foot off the brake my lead dogs were level with her pulling dogs. So the only answer was to stay on the sled and to brake continuously easing the brake when it was soft or uphill.

But now we raced on up the hill and suddenly turned right, finding ourselves back at the Mushers' Lodge but on the wrong side – and the dogs could not be stopped. We needed to be nearer to the kennels. I was out of control and scared. Before I knew what was happening we were racing through the backyard full of kennels, then there was a very unnerving dash as the dogs raced straight out of one area onto the road, which had no snow on it at all, along the road and suddenly, they turned sharp left into the kennels. I was petrified. There was no chance of stopping them or seeing whether any vehicle was coming and with no snow on the road my foot on the brake was of little consequence except to blunt the edges! I just held on praying that I would not fall off and bang my head on the tarmac. As soon as we came into contact with snow, I had my foot hard on the brake. I just wanted to stop and get off. The sled came to a halt; I dug the ice anchor in deep and tied the safety line to something secure. This was the moment we were meant to say a fond farewell to the dogs and thank them for all the work they had done – we would not see them again. I was just thankful that that last awful ride was over and a hot shower was waiting if I was quick. I picked up my rucksack, day bag and sleeping bag from the sled and, without a backward glance in the direction of the dogs, walked away, exhausted, back to the lodge dragging my kit. The only thought going through my head at that moment was 'Done that, been there, never again!' That last part of the trail spiralling down the mountain and back to the lodge had completely finished me off. I never wanted to see a dog-sled again.

Once in the lodge I removed my Arctic suit, gloves, hat and boots and went in search of a refreshing and, hopefully, soothing shower. If Per Thore had been watching this spectacle where I ignored the dogs, maybe he would have changed his mind about whether he would take me on another expedition!

On this last day we had travelled 40 kilometres making a total of nearly two hundred kilometres for the week. It was chaotic as everyone stripped off their Arctic suits, boots, over-mitts, hats and grabbed their wash-kit for a shower. Women first – it had to be quick as we all needed to shower, change into something decent, pack our overnight bag and be ready for 4.30 p.m. Quite a challenge as we only arrived at the Musher's Lodge at 2.00 p.m. Just to complicate matters, another group had arrived at the lodge and, needless to say, were using the bedrooms; and why not? We weren't staying there, we were off for the night to the Ice Palace!

If I thought this trail had been hard, little did I know that this was only a dress rehearsal for a much more difficult trail to come. Although we sled across landscapes covered in a white blanket, I don't think we were ever really that far from civilisation. Within months I would be in the wilderness with just two companions and 26 dogs, all of whom had been bred to run!

Part 3 – The Ice Palace

We were back where we started but there was still another day of the challenge before we were to fly home. We were taken to the Ice Palace and shown around. This was to be where we would sleep that night but before we experienced that, we were taken to a very nice restaurant for a meal. It was a bizarre experience to sleep in a hotel made entirely of ice and drink cocktails out of glasses made of ice.

The following day we experienced a proper Norwegian sauna then, returning to the Musher's Lodge and after fairly minimal instruction, we paired up and tried our skills on snowmobiles. Moira came with me and it didn't take long to get used to driving these big, noisy, smelly vehicles. We drove along frozen rivers and forest paths gradually winding our way up through the woodland until eventually we arrived at the top of a very pretty hill overlooking the town of Kiruna. The view from the top was beautiful – the scenery was made up of scrubby birch and fir trees, a wide frozen river winding its way through the valley amid some relatively low, rounded hills (some topped with snow and some clear of their winter blanket) – a panoramic view in shades of white and grey. The only colour was a hint of blue coming from the sky directly overhead. In the distance it faded into white whilst the sun struggled to make an impact. On the opposite hill was the largest iron ore mine in Europe and it was probably the most unsightly as well – a real blot on such an attractive landscape.

Whilst the view was great (if you avoided the mine), the position we now

Photo 61 — Rona on snowmobile, ready to ride

found ourselves in provided our next challenge – getting down the hill. We had wound our way up to the top but, now, we were heading down in a straight line and our route would take us through lots of scrubby little birch trees. I stopped between two of them, as I followed Taisto down, to find that there was only a thumb width between the snowmobile runners and the trees. As we rounded a bend, the two guys on the snowmobile in front of us, managed to tip it over in the melting snow and Taisto came to their aid not only to get the snowmobile upright again but to take it round the corner for them! I waited expectantly for him to come back to help us – there was a really deep rut of soft snow into which one of their runners had descended and I could see us having exactly the same problem. But I waited in vain, he was out of sight and I was left to negotiate the corner on my own. So very gingerly, Moira and I steered round it through the deep snow. Luckily for Moira I was successful. I allowed myself a little smile as we stayed upright but having negotiated the downhill route we were now back onto frozen water and soon careering along at breakneck speed. It was the inevitable race against the other snowmobiles over the frozen lake.

As we drove along, far over on our left-hand side from high up on the bank there appeared a man on a sled pulled by ten dogs. They raced out of his garden gate and down onto the lake and away in the opposite direction. Suddenly the 'shush' of the sled runners on hardened snow and the pitter patter of the dogs' paws made the snowmobiles seem very loud, noisy, smelly and polluting. They were definitely not nearly as much fun and enjoyable as the sleds. What was I saying?

Back on the trail, the ice was melting and in places the snowmobiles could not keep their grip. In front of us, Sophie and Lucy started to slide backwards towards a big hole. They only just managed to stop and slowly, ever so slowly, start moving forward again. It all looked very scary and Moira and I decided to keep a long, long way away from that area. We travelled on past very old lodges that had been used by travellers for many years in the days when they used horses for transport and then we raced up the next hill and arrived back at the Musher's Lodge. I have to admit, although I was glad I had tried driving snowmobiles, they held no excitement for me at all – give me a dog-sled every time. Was I really saying that? A dog-sled is quieter and it is environmentally friendly and so much more romantic, not to mention that the dogs are such wonderful characters. Where had all this come from? Hadn't I said, not 24 hours earlier, 'Done that, been there, NEVER again!'

Once we were all back at the lodge and the snowmobiles carefully parked, we collected our belongings and were driven to an hotel closer to the airport. Opposite was the local petrol station which we invaded in pursuit of maps so that Per Thore could draw the route we had taken when dog-sledding, for our records. However, I could not fathom out what one of the volunteers was doing. Whilst we had been sledding she had never stopped working and always appeared happiest if she was preparing a meal or washing up. No matter what we said we could not stop her. Mindful that she was heading for home and more fundraising she raided the petrol station for unusual prizes to take with her. However, I am not sure any of us were prepared for the very large cardboard box she appeared with, sealed and labelled for the flight home. It appeared that she had bought up nearly all of the stocks of 'underlay' (the pet name we had given to the flat bread which looked like carpet underlay but tasted delicious that we had for breakfast and for our sandwiches) as well as several wheels of the cheese that we had been devouring all week.

The next day we would be flying home and the adventure would be over but tonight was to be our farewell dinner. Well, it would be for the majority of us. Susan was not at all well and had spent most of the day in bed. She thought the previous night's meal had given her food poisoning but we maintained that, as we had eaten the same meal and were all fighting fit, it may well have been the vodka cocktails that she had devoured at the Ice Palace. However, Susan was not convinced and nothing we said would change her mind. The verdict remains open!

Later that evening we met in the bar for a few drinks before seating ourselves at a long table in the restaurant. On the menu was – yes, you've guessed it – reindeer. Susan managed to join us part way through the meal but she could only manage a very light meal of soup. It was the usual farewell meal and once we had finished eating, Maddy, who is a singer with the group

Steeleye Span, started to sing a song and we all joined in. Soon we were all in full voice and going through an amazing array of songs, so much so that the general public who had come for a quiet meal at the hotel were requesting that we sing various songs that they knew – we did try to oblige as many requests as possible but we had some difficulty remembering a lot of the words.

It was at this meal that the idea of the Nordkapp Expedition started to take place. Oh how fickle can we be?

APPENDIX 3

The Dog Teams

Per Thore's Team

Indigo	Nahini
Jenna	Spretball
Korvo	Barto
Baloo	Scott
Snure	Inuvik

Cathy's Team

Shara	Zita
Youkon	Sira
Tintine	Kusawa
Heiko	Siko

Rona's Team

Vinga	Sally
Snehvit	Varg
Shakira	Creem
Toby	Lucky

APPENDIX 4

Dog-sledding facts

- Each dog has its own harness and its position on the team. The lead dogs are always harnessed and placed on the gang-line (line attached to the sled that goes down the middle of the dogs to which they are attached) first, otherwise the other dogs fret as they do not have leaders.
- When you stop for the day a chain is strung on the ground between two points and from that chain there are shorter chains spaced along its length on which to clip the dogs. The shorter chains are just far enough apart so that the dogs cannot get to each other.
- When you have finished sledding the dogs come off in the reverse order i.e. the dogs nearest the sled come off first and the leaders last.
- Dogs always come first. Water is collected for the dogs' meal before water for the humans. Dogs are fed first.
- The dogs don't drink water so you have to make up a soup of reindeer meat for them to eat to get water inside them, although you will sometimes see them putting their face in the snow as they run as though they were taking snow to eat.
- Once they have had the soup they are given a block of reindeer meat. Along the trails there are lodges. One of the outbuildings will hold a boiler for the water to make the soup. Beside the boiler are large blocks of frozen reindeer meat which look like large bars of chocolate. You take an axe and chop off a cube which is 1 kilo, you then chop this in half and throw that half to the dog. If you hand it to the dog it will bite your fingers off. The frozen block is gone in a flash.
- The dogs' capillaries stop about half an inch or more from the skin so that they do not lose heat. They rest during the summer and eat so that come the autumn they are quite plump. By the spring they are quite skinny through running all winter. They do not enjoy the heat.
- When sledding if you go through soft snow you have to get off and run, pushing the sled to help the dogs.
- When going uphill you have to get off the sled and run pushing the sled to help the dogs.

- You mustn't let the gang-line go slack otherwise the dogs get their paws caught in it and get injured.
- When you are sledding and the dogs turn to the left you have to lean to the left and when they turn to the right you have to lean to the right.
- If you fall you have to keep hold of the sled even if it means being dragged along the trail – you must not let go of the sled. Particularly important if reindeer are near.
- When you stop the sled you have to stamp an 'ice anchor' (metal double hook) into the ice to hold the sled and then tie a line to something secure to hold the sled.

APPENDIX 5

The Route

Sunday

Signaledan – Paras through forest around Barras across Golddajavri to Tri-Nation border and camped.

Monday

Back along trail then up over the Sallorasa Mountains, over the Sallorasa lakes to almost the Finnish border then down and across the road into the forest then on up the mountains to Loassoma cabin near the Finnish border.

Tuesday

Followed Finnish border up in the mountains to the Halti area across Guolasjavri then around the mountains, the wind from the south brought the ground storm over Bidjavaggi (rocky part) then on down to Somas.

Wednesday

Followed the Finnish border to Sidurgoshi – which Per Thore checked out round the Cierte mountains down into the forest, saw reindeer on the Muvraconkka mountains, the roller coaster valley was called Njallaávi then on up and round the Muvasto mountains and followed the reindeer fence posts, had lunch just before lake Sårte javri then crossed the Vuorgu javri then south passed Balgesvarri on to the west of Bastevarri on passed lakes to Goattelvobbäl (ghost city) then into forest and lakes and followed the beginning of the Kautokeino River – followed Kautokeino River and camped near Ak'sumuot'ki.

Thursday

Followed the Kautokeino River under bridge and along then off river to Lappaluobbal (red mountain station but not open) then 9k to Lappuljavri then off across the road a couple of times then a little way up into the Akkarvarri forest until we came to Soussjavri (checkpoint of Finnmark Race).

Friday

On to Lake Soussjavri and river passed Vuotil Mollesjokka (where the Swedish people were) on up to the Mollesjohka Mountain Station (too many people to stop) across the Lesjavri (12km x 8km) the largest lake in Finnmark then down to Jotviak where we rested for a day.

Saturday

Rest day for the dogs.

Sunday

Joatka back towards the lake and then up and round the mountains Stuoranjoas'ki then down to Stabbursdalsjavri (lots of snowmobiles) at north end of lake up into higher ground, straight north until down to Båkkusjavri and camped in Bastinvuobm.

Monday

Followed Bastinjakka (river) then followed the power line trying to get up the east side of Rappes varri – we wanted to get up on high ground but we kept falling so turned down into Gukkesgurro (Valley of Death) across power line – snowmobile trail crossed Dåsggejavri then downhill to Ska'di – across bridge over river and then over the road junction passed hotel – camped beside a lake.

Tuesday

Followed road until drove north along melting river Guorruoag'gi down over mountain but had to turn round as open water Eidavalni – climbed up mountains came to reindeer fences. Saw reindeer near Biereftoajvi. North all the way following the lakes in the Gardevarri. Just before we went to Lavvarjavri (did nosedive) drove round it went through Ruallacåkoaivi climbed up into the mountains then down into Kafjarddalen – not much snow as we came down to Kåjford and camped.

Wednesday

Ryno came – put dogs into trailer and drove through tunnels from island to island past Hennigsvag to Muot'kevarri – once onto the island harnessed the dogs and set off crossing road to Nordkapp and down to Skarsvåg down across the lake following near road all the way to Nordkapp. Nordkapp is on the island of Mageröya.

APPENDIX 6

The Daily Log of The Nordkapp Expedition, April 2004

Day	Position	Weather & Wind	Average Speed	Fastest Speed	Distance covered	Running Total
Sun 11	Tromsø – Drive to Signaldalen		90kph		73k	
Sun 11 p.m.	Tri-Nation Border – Sunnigr 69° 4'N – 20° 34'E	Overcast with light snow flurries.	11.5k	33.3k	25.5k	25.5k
Mon 12	Loassomuvra 69°12'N – 21° E	Sunny – good visibility – getting colder later.	10.3k	27.3k	41k	66.5k
Tues 13	Somas Cabin – Reisa National Park – 69°17'N – 21°30'E	Sunny to begin with then very windy in Finland to extremely windy -25°C at Halti Mountains.	10.3k	25k	48k	114.5k
Wed 14	Oaddgeteekke 76°55'N – 22°36'E	Sunny and very cold to start then cloudy and finally overcast with intermittent sunshine. Sunny at lunch.	10.4k	18k	90k	204.5k
Thurs 15	Sossjavri 76°17'N – 23°30'E	Very sunny, clouded over in the afternoon.	9.3k	26.1k	75k	279.5k
Fri 16	Jotkajavrre 69°45'N – 23°56'E	Overcast all day – sun trying to break through.	10.5k	28.5k	57k	336.5k
Sat 17		Rest day for the dogs				
Sun 18	Bestinvvobm 70°6'N – 24°9'E	Overcast – low cloud, -1°C.	8.2k	19.6k	48k	384.5k

Day	Position	Weather & Wind	Average Speed	Fastest Speed	Distance covered	Running Total
Mon 19	Ska'di 70°26'N – 24°30'E	Overcast	10.1k	21.7k	54k	438.5k
Tues 20	Kafjord 71°52'N – 25°45'E	Sunny, crisp.	10.2k	26.5k	81k	519.5k
Wed 21	Nordkapp – 13.50	Light wind, light cloudy, grey sky to the North –rain over the sea.	7k	10k	13k	532.5k
Thurs 22	Honnigsvåg – Tromsø by Cruise Ship					

APPENDIX 7

The Sámi People

The Sámi people are an indigenous race of people who roam from Hedmark in Norway across Sweden and Finland to the Kola peninsula of Russia. There are thought to be about 70,000 Sámi people, their name is derived from Sápmi which is the name of their territory. Because the Sámi region covers such a wide variation in culture and economics, the Sámi societies are very diverse. The Sámi language, traditional clothing, handicraft and music are very different from the other ethnic minorities in Scandinavia. Due to the diversity of the societies and the nature of the language, new words are often evolved.

The Sámi people have developed an economy which has a direct relationship to nature and the natural resources available. Often called the 'reindeer people', some Sámi follow the reindeer herds and by law are allowed land and water rights. Other Sámi live by the coast and concentrate on fishing, but all hunt and follow the crafts. However due to their land being reduced by mining and the cutting down of the forests many Sámi follow other careers as well. In the winter the 'reindeer people' can be found in the lowlands but as spring arrives the reindeer move up towards the mountains and a few of the menfolk follow them to take care of them. Once the herds are up in the mountains then fences are erected to stop the reindeer moving back down to the lowlands thus giving the pastures time to rejuvenate. The reindeer carry their calves from Sept/Oct and they are born in the late Spring May/June when the snow has melted a little and there is more food so that the mothers can produce more milk.

Every part of the reindeer is used. The animal is used for transport, the cows are milked, the skins are used to make the coneshaped 'tents' *Laitok/ Lavvu* and clothes, the tendons and sinews for sewing shoes and clothing and even the intestines are utilised as they provide much needed vitamins for the Sámi people. The cut marks on the reindeer's ear denotes who it belongs to.

It is believed that the Sámi people were the first to travel along the coasts after the Ice Age. Up until the 15th Century the Sámi were hunter/gatherers but during the century they started to tame the reindeer herds and became nomads. However, with the increasing industrialisation their lifestyle began to disappear. The number of people who can sustain a living from tending the reindeer is diminishing and many Sámi have been integrated into the mainstream society.

(http://arcticcircle.uconn.edu/HistoryCulture/Sámiindex.html)

The author acknowledges that this material was taken from internet sources and does not claim authorship of this brief history of the Sámi people.

APPENDIX 8

The Team CVs

Per Thore

Background
Per Thore Hansen is Norwegian from Skutvik, 37 years old, married with two children aged 7 and 2. After finishing College he joined the Army, serving in the Norwegian Special Forces as a Paratrooper for seven years, spending 2 years in Lebanon, 6 months in Bosnia and 3 months in Somalia. He was in the Norwegian National Team for Cross Country Skiing when he joined the Army. When he left the Army he took a course to become a social worker and led a programme for children with drug problems. Per Thore is happier with a team of huskies in the mountains than in an office. In the winter months he guides tourists as they dog-sled around the mountains in Sweden and Norway.

Dog Sledding Expeditions
In 2000 Per Thore took part in the Finnmark Race, the longest and hardest race in Europe covering 1000 kilometres.

In 2001 he took part in the Fjellreven Polar Race, 350 kilometres from Norway to Sweden in which he finished second.

In 2002 he took part in the Fjellreven Polar Race again, this time winning it and in 2003 he was third.

Why does Per Thore want to spend two weeks crossing 650 kilometres of Arctic wilderness behind a team of dogs?
'I have always wanted to do this expedition and it is only now that I will be in a position to take time out of my normal working life to explore this beautiful area of Norway. This time I will not be racing and we will be far away from snowmobiles and 21st-century traffic, at one with the environment.'

Rona Cant

Background

Rona Cant is British, divorced with two grown-up children and lives in Oxford.

Rona has a Diploma in Private Secretaryship and graduated with a BA Hons in English and Geography from Oxford Brookes University in 1998.

Her first book *A Challenge Too Far?* was published in October 2003. It is the story of Rona's experience of the BT Global Challenge Round the World Yacht Race 2000–2001 – The World's Toughest Yacht Race.

Rona runs her own company helping organisations across the world understand what works and what doesn't work in leadership and teamwork or how by thinking differently you can overcome obstacles and challenges. She is Managing Director of Arctic Leadership Challenges Ltd. where she works alongside Per Thore to take Senior Executives into the Arctic Circle for personal development – dog-sledding in March and sailing from mid-June to mid-August giving them a chance to learn the lessons from extreme expeditions but in a safe environment.

Adventures

Rona decided to abandon her old way of life and seek the adventure she had always craved.

Rona successfully circumnavigated the world in the BT Global Challenge Round the World Yacht Race 2000–2001 despite a major crash in Wellington.

In July 2001 Rona trekked the West Coast Trail on Vancouver Island, one of the ten toughest trails in the world; a distance of 77k.

In April 2003 Rona was on the winning yacht in the Round Britain Challenge.

Adventure detail

Rona started sailing in 1994 and after a total of one month's sailing had an interview with Sir Chay Blyth for the BT Global Challenge. She was one of 180 out of 4–5,000 applicants to gain a place on the Race, 15% of whom were to drop out and need replacing. The route was the 'wrong way' round the world i.e. against the prevailing winds and currents and was that first sailed by Sir Chay Blyth 30 years earlier.

Two days after returning from the race Rona flew to Canada to embark on her next adventure. The West Coast Trail is also known as the Shipwreck Trail and it takes ten hours to cover 10k. Rona met the bears at the beginning of the trail, met the Indians and had the company of a cougar as she waited to be evacuated out due to damage to her knee brought on by lack of time to recover from the Global.

Rona was successful in the selection process to gain a place on the Round Britain Challenge and utilised the skills learnt on the Global Challenge to help win the race.

Rona was brought up with dogs when as a small child her father bred Cocker Spaniels. The kennel lad would take Rona and her sister for a walk (on reins) when he walked the puppies. When she was a teenager her family once more had dogs and whereas the family dogs have been gentle Rona bears the scars of being attacked by a pack of Jack Russells in her mid-teens.

Why does Rona want to spend two weeks crossing 650 kilometres of Arctic wilderness behind a team of dogs?

'I spent my 20s+ years wanting to travel but not having the confidence to fulfil my ambitions. Getting divorced and graduating showed me that I could do anything that I turned my mind to. I do not ski so going fast over icy/ snowy ground is overcoming my innermost fears – pushing my boundaries, challenging myself. My father always believed that his daughters could do anything they wanted to – he who did it best did it.

I believe men and women to be equal, they just have different strengths and weaknesses and the adventures that I have done have proven that. As if reflecting life, women are beginning to reach the top in sailing and in climbing.

To experience a different culture, one where dog-sledding is the norm, will be fascinating. To learn to read the weather in snowy conditions will be interesting and to have to rely on ourselves in the wilderness where the terrain will be tough will make this an expedition where fitness and stamina will play a major role. Cathy and I are both strong characters and to see how we relate in the close confines of a tent in sub-zero temperatures when we are cold, exhausted and hungry will be an interesting exercise. Whereas on the Global it was always the boat that came first, this time it will be the dogs no matter how we feel.

Cathy O'Dowd

Background

Cathy O'Dowd is a South African, 35 years old, married but without children, living in Andorra. She was raised and educated in South Africa, moving to Europe in 2000 to pursue her interest in adventure.

Cathy has a Masters Degree in Media Studies from Rhodes University.

She has written two books, both about Everest. *Everest: Free To Decide* was co-written with Ian Woodall. *Just for the love of it* is Cathy's story of her first three Everest expeditions.

Cathy works as a professional speaker, sharing with corporations her lessons learnt from Everest about teamwork and motivation. She has spoken in 22 countries on 5 continents.

Climbing

Cathy has been climbing mountains for 17 years, throughout southern and central Africa, in South America, in the Alps and in the Himalayas. She remains an active mountaineer, rock-climber and skier.

In 1996 Cathy became the first South African to climb Everest, and in 1999 the first woman in the world to climb Everest from both south and north sides.

In 2000 she became the fourth woman to climb Lhotse, the world's fourth highest mountain.

In spring 2003 Cathy attempted to climb a new route on the notorious east face of Everest. This ambitious project was ultimately unsuccessful.

Everest detail

Cathy was one of 200 women who applied for a place on the famous, and controversial, 1st South African Everest Expedition of 1996, and was the one finally selected. The team followed the Edmund Hillary route, fighting their way through 'the worst storm in Everest's history'. Despite being the apprentice on the team, and having to deal with three fellow team members walking out, on 25 May 1996 Cathy reached the summit. It was, however, a tough introduction, as a team-mate was killed on the descent.

In 1998 Cathy took on the challenge of the treacherous north side of Everest, where George Mallory had famously disappeared in 1924. Her attempt ended when she stopped to try and save a dying American woman. In 1999 Cathy returned once more, and succeeded, becoming the first woman in the world to climb Everest from both north and south sides.

Post-Everest

After four expeditions to Everest, Cathy is swearing 'no more Everest' and looking for new challenges to tackle.

Cathy's entire experience with dogs consists of owning a Pomeranian, which, with all the imagination of an eight-year-old, she called Fluffy. The Pomeranian had an illicit affair with a poodle in the park, and produced two puppies, adding Wassit and Tapocita to Cathy's dog team. The most Cathy ever managed to get them to do was to run round the garden in circles, yapping.

Why does Cathy want to spend two weeks crossing 650 kilometres of Arctic wilderness behind a team of dogs?

'Having spent much of my time on foot, humping heavy loads up snowy slopes, I am fascinated by this ancient form of travel, by the bond of trust and courage and shared aim that must exist between person and dog to travel together successfully.

Adventure is a very macho field, heavily dominated by men. And virtually all of my climbing has been done with men. To work together closely with another woman is an additional element of this challenge.

The psychological challenge is as interesting as the physical one. I want to know if I have got what it takes to complete this adventure, and to do so in a spirit of friendship and good humour. I have seen many teams crack under the pressures of the wilderness. I hope that Rona and I have the experience, and the temperament, to meet whatever we may encounter with grace.

Glossary

Gang-line — Wire line that goes from the sled to the back harness line of the front dogs. All the dogs are attached to it from the back of their harness and at the front to their collars

Brake — A piece of metal with a spoke at each end which is attached to the sled and has an elasticated cord attached to it so that it is normally raised but you have to put your foot firmly on it to stop the sled.

Snowmobile brake — A mat that fits between the runners at the back of the sled made of rubber similar to the tracks on a snowmobile which you stand on to slow the sled down. When not in use it is held up against the back of the sled with a piece of bungee cord.

Ice Anchor — This is like a metal handle with two large curved spokes on it which you stamp into the ground to hold the sled if you want to get off the runners without the dogs haring off over the horizon.

Mushing — Putting one foot onto the snow as we went along to help push the sled up the hill – a little like scooting.

Runners — Two pieces of wood either side of the sled, which protrude out of the back. This is where you stand. They help the sled to go over the terrain.

Moguls — Small mounds of snow – similar to very steep road-humps

Puke — A sled pulled by a skier using a harness round the waist.